Heroes with Heart

Heroes with Heart

*Canadian Athletes
You Can Look Up To*

Steve Proctor / Dahlia Reich / Beverley Ware

WINDING
STAIR
PRESS

Cataloguing in Publication Data is available.

ISBN 1-55366-304-7

Winding Stair Press
An imprint of Stewart House Publishing Inc.
290 North Queen Street, #210
Toronto, Ontario, M9C 5K4
Canada
1-866-574-6873
www.stewarthousepub.com

Developmental Editor: Judy Phillips
Text Design: Laura Brady
Cover Design: Darrin Laframboise
Photo Research: Jane Affleck

This book is available at special discounts for bulk purchases by groups or organizations for sales promotions, premiums, fundraising and educational purposes. For details, contact: Stewart House Publishing Inc., Special Sales Department, 195 Allstate Parkway, Markham, Ontario L3R 4T8. Toll free 1-866-474-3478.

1 2 3 4 5 6   07 06 05 04 03 02

Printed in Canada

To the family and friends of the 31 athletes profiled in this book. Your unflinching support and quiet sacrifices nurture them, so they can inspire us.

The Line Up

Acknowledgements

Like a top athlete who depends on friends, family, colleagues and coaches to reach the top, *Heroes with Heart* drew on the skills of many talented people to get to press.

Among the most important were Dahlia Reich of London, Ontario, and Beverley Ware of Halifax, Nova Scotia, who shared the task of tracking down the athletes and telling their awe-inspiring stories in fresh and engaging ways. They dedicate this book to their own budding athletes, Dahlia's Jonas, Graeme, and Gabrielle; and Beverley's Breanna, Nicholas, and Gregory. The efforts of Steve Maich who produced two wonderful profiles, and the advice offered by Laurent LePierres, cannot be underestimated. Jane Affleck deserves kudos for her photo research as does Darrin Laframboise for the cover design. The clean, crisp design of the book is thanks to the good work of Laura Brady. At Stewart House Publishing, the support and talents of Ken Proctor and Joe March brought the book to life.

Arranging interviews with the athletes while they crisscrossed the globe was not always easy. Thanks go to Mary Lynn Jenkins, Sharon Podatt at Landmark Sport Group, and posthumously to Chook Maxwell for helping facilitate interviews and digging up much-needed information.

None of it could have been possible without the support of my wife Deborah and my daughters, Cydney and Mackenzie.

Steve Proctor

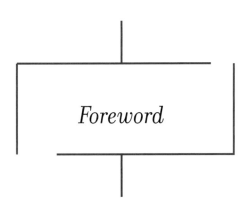

Foreword

In these pages are stories about heroes . . . athletes who shine brightly for their achievements in sport and their contributions to the world around them. These are athletes whose achievements are overshadowed by the journeys they took to get to the podium and the journeys they continue on today at home in their communities. These are the stories of everyday Canadians who do amazing things. All of them share common traits . . . hard work, persistence, and determination. That seems to be the recipe for winning . . . just stir and add water. As you'll read in Trevor Linden's story, even his dad, Lance, knew his son was never the best on the team. But what young Trevor did possess, as Lance describes, was "a determination that was

unparalleled." Little wonder that Trevor is making his living in the NHL today.

These stories prove that you don't need to be the biggest or the strongest to succeed. It's all about heart and will. That's what separates these great athletes from mere mortals. If you want inspiration, each story has some of that. Who can't be inspired by Olympian Rick Hansen, who says, "Success is not measured by whether you use your legs or not, it's how you live your life."

The other universal truth from almost all the athletes is that it isn't about winning Stanley Cups or Olympic medals. It is about the journey. Aiming to be the best, enjoying the thrill of competition, loving the training, conquering one's fears, pushing on through injuries. This is the ultimate test—to be the best you can be . . . a cliché yes, but so true.

After reading the stories, you'll marvel at how none of the athletes' successes came easily. There were hurdles and obstacles all the way and usually injuries to battle at the worst possible time. Whether it was Silken Laumann or Elvis Stojko, the athlete somehow was able to draw on a will so strong that he or she forgot about the pain and pushed forward. That single-mindedness is impressive. When Laumann won the bronze medal at the 1992 Olympics after having her leg ripped apart just weeks before in a training accident, that bronze was better than gold—just racing was a huge victory.

The other thing I was struck by was how so many athletes are giving back. They are involved in charities and organizations where they are just as determined to make a difference in the lives of others. Maybe it's that Canadian

"niceness," but, from Wayne Gretzky to Lorie Kane, they are sharing the benefits they've reaped in sports to help others.

We need to read these stories. We need to share them and celebrate them. We need to remember that the determination and heart found in these athletes' stories you are about to read is in each and every one of us. For those of you involved in sports, there are many lessons to be learned in the following pages. Tap into some of your inner strength and find out what you can become. For the rest of us, just read and marvel that ordinary Canadians can do extraordinary things.

Enjoy it and be inspired. I know I was.

Colleen Jones

Colleen Jones
FOUR-TIME NATIONAL
CURLING CHAMPION
2001 WORLD CHAMPION

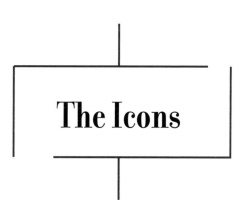

The Icons

Wayne Gretzky
Still the Great One

BORN: JANUARY 26, 1961
BRANTFORD, ONTARIO

When Wayne Gretzky was 10 years old, his father, Walter, pulled him aside after a terrible game and blasted him. "You can't play a bad game," he yelled. "People are going to judge you on how you perform every night. Never forget that." And the best the NHL has ever seen seldom did. During a 20-year career that made him the most famous Canadian on the planet, Gretzky repeatedly earned the title "The Great One"—not just for the phenomenal number of goals he scored and games he won, but for his gentlemanly, ever humble, quintessentially Canadian style.

He played the game as Canadians imagined it should be played. He worked hard, regardless of whether it was a practice or a Stanley Cup final. He was the ultimate team player, who valued his assists more than his goals and club victories more than either. He remained humble, self-deprecating, and upbeat, and never allowed anyone to make him bigger than the game.

Still baby-faced at age 41, it's been almost four years since he played his last official NHL game. Yet Gretzky remains at centre ice in the hockey world. He served as the unpaid executive director of Canada's 2002 men's Olympic hockey team, is the man with the final say on all on-ice decisions for the Phoenix Coyotes, and has been the role model to millions of kids who drag their overstuffed hockey bags into frigid arenas.

And number 99 has left big skates for them to fill. He learned to skate at age two and within four years he was playing against players twice his age. By age 10, he'd notched 369 career goals. That total climbed to more than 1,000 before the "skinny kid from Brantford" joined the WHA's Indianapolis Racers at the age of 17 and began to rewrite the hockey record book.

After taking hockey to new and dizzying heights during his 20-year career, Gretzky retired, holding or sharing 61 NHL records (40 for regular season, 15 for Stanley Cup playoffs, and 6 for all-star games). He helped win four Stanley Cup championships and three Canada Cup tournament titles. He remains the NHL's all-time leading goal, assist, and point producer for both regular season and playoffs. You can see his name engraved on the Hart Trophy as the League's MVP, twice on the Conn Smythe Trophy as playoff MVP, and five times on the Lady Byng Trophy as the NHL's most gentlemanly player.

He is ranked as the number one player in the history of the NHL—just ahead of Bobby Orr and his personal idol, Gordie Howe—and was selected as the Canadian Press Male Athlete of the Century. He is the only player in the history of the NHL to have his jersey number retired by all member clubs. In an early 2002 national public opinion poll, he was identified as the greatest living Canadian of the 20th century.

Yet with all his awards and a slew of goals that made history, when asked about his greatest contribution to the game before his induction into the Hockey Hall of Fame on November 22,

Edmonton Oiler hockey great Wayne Gretzky screams with joy as he hoists the Stanley Cup over his head following the team's win over the New York Islanders in Edmonton, May 19, 1984.

1999, he didn't talk about lifting the Cup over his head for the first time or how his star power brought in a new generation of fans to the game. He said simply that he hoped he'd paved the way for young players who, like himself in his earlier days, were told they weren't big enough, fast enough, or strong enough.

"I'm probably someone kids can look to and say, 'Well, he made it. Maybe I can make it,'" he said with trademark modesty. And struggling players with big dreams really can take heart. Despite the fact he revolutionized hockey and even elevated the performance of other legends like Jari Kurri, Paul Coffey, and Mark Messier, Gretzky wasn't especially fast, nor was his shot exceedingly strong. Analysts agree on that and the fact that Gretzky, with his slender frame—he's six feet one inch and weighs 170 pounds— was no hockey player prototype.

But he was smart. Like a chess grand master, he saw patterns in the game more than individual plays. Helmet low and his body bent at the waist, he didn't go to where the puck was. He went to where he knew it was going. "Gretzky sees a game out there that no one else sees," former Boston Bruins coach and general manger Harry Sinden once told *The Hockey News* as he struggled to explain Gretzky's success.

Whether at the office, at a restaurant, or now on the golf courses he loves, Gretzky always makes time for fans. He signs thousands of hats, sticks, and other memorabilia at charity events with a shy, slightly embarrassed grin

that says he doesn't think he deserves the recognition. Many a team bus has been late because Gretzky lagged behind, trying to sign a few more autographs for fans.

With his own clothing line, equity ownership positions in two restaurants (Wayne Gretzky's in Toronto and

Wayne Gretzky, spokesman for TransAlta's Project Planet Challenge, signs autographs for kids following an awards ceremony in Edmonton, October 5, 2001. The project asks school kids to come up with environmental and educational programs. (CP Photo / Edmonton Sun—Brendon Dlouhy)

the All-Star Café in New York), and numerous corporate clients, Gretzky could make more off his career as a pitchman than he ever earned holding a hockey stick.

But his days are not all about endorsements and photo shoots. He lends his name and image freely to assist charitable causes and is an active participant in educational programs. The Great One has personally dropped thousands of medals around the necks of starry-eyed young skaters as part of the Esso Medal of Achievement program. He is involved with Ronald McDonald Children's Charities, and some Canadians wake up to the Great One's face on cans of Folgers coffee as part of a pitch to raise money for the Boys and Girls Clubs of Canada.

As an ambassador for Project Planet, an environmental education program that challenges students to come up with practical projects to improve the environment, Gretzky not only promotes the cause with classroom visits but also helps winning students make their projects become a reality. After an unannounced Project Planet visit with 500 excited elementary students at Vincent Massey School in Ottawa, Gretzky said that while talking hockey with the kids is fun, it's more important to teach them about the environment. "I'm a parent and it's amazing what we learn from our kids. What kids bring home raises so much awareness in other family members."

In recent years he's been able to combine his charitable work with perfecting his golf swing. The Wayne Gretzky and Friends Invitational has been held in Nova Scotia for the past two years and has raised more than $100,000 for P.E.B.B.L.E.S., a unique technology project initiated by Gretzky that's designed to provide two-way audiovisual communication between classrooms and hospitalized students.

Gretzky lives in sunny Los Angeles with Janet Jones, a former actress, and his four children, but he has never forgotten his small-town Canadian roots. He talks frequently and passionately about learning to skate at age two on the Nith River near Brantford and the hours he spent honing his skills in a backyard rink. His desire to skate was so strong, he recalls in his 1990 autobiography, that he ate many dinners with his skates on, just so he wouldn't have to waste the time lacing up.

When Gretzky was traded to Los Angeles from Edmonton in 1988—in one of the biggest deals in sports history—some Canadian hockey fans wept, believing they had lost a national treasure. Letters to the editor in newspapers across the country were filled with irate rants and mournful laments from ordinary Canadians who saw the trade as a blow to our national identity, a rip in the very fabric of Canada.

But the move was ultimately good for hockey and paved the way for the success of the league in the sunbelt. And really, Gretzky was never very far from home. He sported the Maple Leaf in four Canada Cup tournaments and fulfilled a lifetime dream when he donned a red-and-white jersey to play for Canada at the 1998 Olympics at Nagano, Japan. The dream turned into something of a nightmare when he was passed over by coach Marc Crawford in the shootout loss to the Czech Republic and the team finished out of the medal race, but the Great One still got a shot at Olympic redemption.

Under pressure to deliver gold and despite his lack of experience on the general-management side of hockey matters, Gretzky built a team for the Salt Lake City Olympics that combined youth and experience. There was a bump or two along the way, but ultimately the 23 players he hand-picked for the job brought the country to its collective feet when it claimed Canada's first gold medal in men's hockey in half a century.

The win was sweet for Gretzky, but afterwards he refused to talk about himself as a key part of the gold medal victory. "I'm really happy for Canadians," he said repeatedly with a wide smile bursting across his face. "I'm very proud of our players and coaches—they deserve all the credit."

We know better.

This athlete supports:
P.E.B.B.L.E.S.
c/o Ryerson Polytechnic University
Centre for Learning Technologies
Room W373
350 Victoria Street
Toronto, ON M5B 2K3

Ken Dryden
Backstopping Education

BORN: AUGUST 8, 1947
TORONTO, ONTARIO

In 1970, when Ken Dryden received the offer to play pro hockey for the Montreal Canadiens, he accepted on one condition. He didn't want more money or a guarantee that he wouldn't be traded. Instead, Ken Dryden wanted the team's promise that he would be allowed to complete his law degree at Montreal's McGill University.

For thousands of young Canadians, receiving an offer to play pro hockey, especially for a team as storied as the Montreal Canadiens, would be a dream come true. But Ken Dryden never wanted to be just another hockey player. A commitment to schooling was always a driving force in Dryden's life, and the mere fact that he was being handed the chance to play pro hockey wasn't going to blunt his dedication. If he couldn't continue with his education, then hockey could wait.

Even then, at 23 years of age, Ken Dryden knew the fame and lightning-quick reflexes of a professional hockey player fade with time, but that education lasts a lifetime. As it turned out, Dryden's talent in goal was so undeniable that the Canadiens' management would have agreed to almost any condition to get the goalie's signature on a contract.

Drafted by the Boston Bruins in 1964 at age 17, Dryden's rights were traded to Montreal later the same year in exchange for two players who would never play in the NHL. But pro hockey was still far from Dryden's thoughts. It was just a way to earn a top-notch education at a minimal cost. He attended Cornell University, the highly regarded U.S. college in Ithaca, New York, where he earned his bachelor's degree. He also played hockey for Cornell, where he became an all-American, and Montreal's scouts soon realized that they had a genuine star on their hands.

In three years with Cornell University Dryden perfected the stand-up style of goaltending that would make him the greatest in the game. He used his six-foot four-inch, 200-pound frame to fill the net and intimidate shooters. In three years at the school, Dryden amassed the stunning record of 76 wins, 4 losses, and one tie. His goals against average of 1.59 helped make Cornell the most dominant college team of that era.

After Cornell, Dryden played two seasons with the Canadian National Team before Montreal came calling and Dryden struck his unusual deal. The Canadiens would allow Dryden the flexibility in his schedule to attend law classes at McGill then rush across town

Former Montreal Canadiens goaltender Ken Dryden rests on his stick during a 1979 game.

in time for practice with Montreal's minor-league affiliate, The Voyageurs.

As it turned out, Dryden played only half a season for the Voyageurs before being called up to the Canadiens. He started six regular-season games for Montreal and won them all. When the team prepared to enter the playoffs, the coaches had a tough decision. Montreal's regular goaltender, Rogie Vachon, had played inconsistently for much of the season. In the end, coach Al MacNeil shocked the hockey world by benching Vachon and anointing Dryden Montreal's starting goaltender.

MacNeil's faith in the young man paid huge dividends. Dryden was spectacular, winning the Conn Smythe Trophy as the most valuable player of the postseason as he led the Canadiens to a Stanley Cup victory over the Chicago Blackhawks. It was just weeks into his NHL career, and Dryden was being hailed as one of the best goalies in the world.

But that Stanley Cup victory wasn't just an important beginning for Dryden; it marked the start of perhaps the greatest dynasty in pro sports history. The Montreal Canadiens of the 1970s, dubbed the "Flying Frenchmen," won six Stanley Cups and boasted such future Hall of Famers as Guy LaFleur, Serge Savard, Henri Richard, Larry Robinson, and Yvon Cournoyer. They were rich, young, famous, and absolutely adored by legions of fans in Quebec.

For a time, as the champagne flowed and money rolled in, it seemed as though the good times would never end. But Dryden knew better. He quickly developed a reputation as a

Ken Dryden, president of the Maple Leaf Hockey Club, points out features of the Air Canada Centre to 100-year-old Bessie Lamson, wearing a Toronto Maple Leafs jersey with the number 100. Lamson started working at Maple Leaf Gardens in 1931, as a concession vendor. She served the first hotdog at Maple Leaf Gardens but quit in the mid-1940s because she wasn't allowed to listen to Leaf games on the radio while she worked.

loner, as he diligently continued his studies. He could often be found sitting alone on team flights and bus rides, his head buried deep in a huge textbook, preparing for an upcoming law exam or jotting down notes for an essay.

But his concentration on schoolwork didn't hurt Dryden's goaltending. His stellar debut that helped Montreal win the Stanley Cup in 1971 was followed by another outstanding year in 1972. According to league rules, Dryden hadn't played enough in the 1971 regular season to be considered for the honour of "rookie of the year," but he claimed the award that following season, recording 39 wins, 8 losses, 8 shutouts, and a 2.24 goals-against average.

Yet, all his remarkable success on the ice never seemed quite real to Dryden. In his book, *The Game,* published in 1983, Dryden recalled the surprise he felt at his sudden celebrity. "I thought the Canadiens would simply take over from my parents for a time, paying my tuition and books, my room and board, and little else until I graduated. Then, after giving them one more year, as I was obliged to do, I would merely stop playing and they would stop paying," he wrote. "But I was better than we both thought."

Much better indeed. Dryden played goal for Canada's team that took on the Soviet Union in the famous 1972 Summit Series. It was a tough series for Canada. Widely expected to trounce the little-known Soviets, the Canadians had to fight a mighty struggle. They finally won on Paul Henderson's climactic goal late in the final game in Moscow. Dryden's great play in the final period of that final game gave the Canadian team the chance it needed to win. And Dryden, like all the other members of that famous 1972 squad, has become legendary for his part in the gutsy, come-from-behind victory.

Following the summit series, Montreal won yet another Stanley Cup in 1972–3. That season, Dryden won his first Vezina Trophy as the NHL's top goaltender. It was then that Dryden's career took its sharpest turn, and his commitment to education was tested. After winning two Stanley cups and the Conn Smythe, Calder, and Vezina Trophies—all in his first three years in the league—Dryden expected a substantial raise when it came time to renegotiate

his contract. But in those days before free agency and huge player contracts, Montreal refused to pay Dryden what he demanded. Rather than sign for less than he felt he was worth, Dryden walked away from the game and turned his attention to completing his law degree full time.

Rather than making thousands of dollars per week playing goal for hockey's best team, Dryden chose to finish his degree as an articling clerk at a Toronto law firm for $137 a week. To many, the idea that a pro athlete would leave the game at the peak of his career, giving up celebrity status to make far less money in an anonymous job, was ludicrous. But in *The Game,* Dryden explains that money was never the driving factor in his life. "Money can be a trap," he writes. "For what happens later? What happens to the lifestyle, the expectations, the lawyer, accountant, and investment counselor, the respect and self-respect when the money stops? And it will stop." He knew, even then, that his law degree would be more important in his life than any one hockey season.

In 1974, Dryden and the Canadiens reconciled, and the game's best goaltender returned to the ice. For the next five seasons, Dryden backstopped one of the greatest teams ever to four Stanley Cups. Dryden was named to the NHL first all-star team four more times and won the Vezina Trophy four more times.

In 1979, at the relatively young age of 32, and after playing only seven full seasons in the NHL, Dryden hung up his skates again, this time for good. But the end of Dryden's hockey career really marked the beginning of what has been an even more important string of achievements.

Shortly after retiring from the NHL, Dryden wrote the book *Home Game,* and it was quickly recognized as one of the finest books ever written about Canada's national obsession. It was later made into a documentary series for the Canadian Broadcasting Corporation, for which Dryden received two Gemini Awards, the highest honour in Canadian television production.

He followed up *Home Game* with *The Game,* a closer examination of the later years in his own career and the waning days of Montreal's Flying Frenchmen dynasty. The book was a finalist for the Governor General's Literary Award, one of the most significant awards for Canadian literature. It soon became clear from his writing that Dryden was far more than an ex-jock scrib-

bling his memoirs for the benefit of a few thousand sports fans. These were serious discussions of some of the deeper issues in Canada and in sport. Ken Dryden the writer and academic had far more to offer than a retelling of his favourite kick saves.

By the time Dryden was inducted into the Hockey Hall of Fame in 1983, his influence beyond the sporting world was expanding. The bestseller success of Dryden's first books paved the way for him to become a respected advocate for his two life-long passions: education and sports.

Two universities, the University of Moncton, in New Brunswick, and Queen's University, in Kingston, Ontario, commissioned Dryden to study and make recommendations to improve their varsity sports programs. Both schools had come to be concerned that their sports programs weren't offering the proper balance between academic and athletic achievement. Dryden is credited at both schools with helping to foster great strides in this area.

Dryden was also invited to be a consultant for the National Commission on Education, making recommendations to the Canadian government, as well as provincial governments, as to how to improve the school system. That project led to yet another bestselling book, 1995's *In School: Our Kids, Our Teachers, Our Classrooms,* in which he describes and reflects on the year he spent in an Ontario school shadowing students, attending classes, and getting to know teachers, administrators, pupils, and their parents.

In 1997, Dryden made his return to the NHL, this time as president of the Toronto Maple Leafs. Much of his professional life is now dedicated to bringing the Stanley Cup back to Toronto, and he has presided over an era of vast improvement in the team. But he hasn't left behind his commitment to children and the opportunities that are unlocked in the classroom. It was that commitment that led, in large part, to his 1999 induction into the International Scholar-Athlete Hall of Fame.

The insights he has gained over the years into the ways children learn and teachers teach have stoked Dryden's beliefs. They drove him to establish the Ken Dryden Scholarship program, for Canadian children in the child welfare system, with the National Youth in Care Network. The scholarships are awarded each year to several students, living in group-homes or with foster families, who show special potential for success at college or university. The scholarships provide up to $3,000 per student to defray the costs of tuition and fees that can often stand in the way of under-privileged kids, preventing them from fulfilling their potential.

"Two of my favourite times of the year have to do with the scholarship," Dryden said recently. "The first is when I read all the applications and I'm able to share the incredible, inspiring, life-affirming stories each represents. These young people don't realize just how much they have achieved, and just how ready they are to achieve lots more. The second is when I make the phone calls to inform the winners, when I'm able to hear the voices of people who deserve everything they get, actually getting what they deserve."

This athlete supports:

National Youth in Care Network

20-99 Fifth Avenue

Ottawa, ON K1S 5K4

website: www.youthincare.ca

Terry Fox
The Marathon Continues

BORN: JULY 28, 1958
WINNIPEG, MANITOBA
DIED JUNE 28, 1981, AT AGE 22

Today, we got up at 4:00 a.m. As usual, it was tough . . . If I died, I would die happy because I was doing what I wanted to do. How many people could say that? I went out and did 15 push-ups in the road and took off. My head was light but the double-sightedness went away. At five miles, Doug [Alward, driver and good friend] and I talked about it for a while. I cried because I knew I was going to make it or be in a hospital bed or dead. I want to set an example that will never be forgotten.

—TERRY FOX, DAY 15 OF HIS MARATHON OF HOPE.

And so he did, across our nation and around the world. It was April 12, 1980, when Terry Fox dipped his artificial leg in the harbour at St. John's, Newfoundland, and launched his dream of running across Canada to raise money for cancer research. He was 21 years old.

The journey would end abruptly, 5,373 kilometres after it began, but the dream would survive. In 143 days, Terry Fox set an example that indeed will never be forgotten, an example that, to this day, is a beacon for hope, humanitarianism, and the human spirit. The magnitude of the Terry Fox legacy is astounding. He is a Canadian legend, his story our proudest piece of history. Incredibly, his impact grows more profound every year, bringing together millions of people around the world to share in his lesson of limitless determination and in the battle against a common foe.

Terry Fox set out that April day with the hope of raising one dollar for every Canadian in the fight against cancer. To date, his dream has brought in nearly $300 million worldwide and has become the cornerstone of numerous cancer research breakthroughs that have saved or prolonged countless lives. "He would be smiling if he knew," says Darrell Fox, Terry's younger brother and national director of the Terry Fox Foundation. "If he only knew."

Canadian pride, in a humble young man who set out to accomplish the impossible, is evident in all that carries his name—parks, playgrounds, highways, walkways, streets, schools, scholarships, awards, monuments, stamps, a plane, a mountain peak, a ship, even an iceberg, and much more. But this would not make Terry smile. "He would be uncomfortable," claims Darrell. "He thought that anything he did, everyone else was capable of doing, if only they put their mind to it and tried their very best. His story still moves people because it's a story of an average person attempting the extraordinary. It's a story of how one person can make a difference."

The story begins in Port Coquitlam, B.C., where Betty and Rolly Fox were raising four active children—Fred, Terry, Darrell, and Judith. Terry in particular was a sports enthusiast, a gutsy kid who was relentless in all his pursuits. At the end of his first year at Simon Fraser University, Terry began feeling a pain in his knee, which he thought was from playing basketball. It was much worse. Terry was diagnosed with osteogenic sarcoma, a rare, malignant tumour, and on March 9, 1977, his leg was amputated six inches above the knee.

The night before his operation, Terry read an article about an amputee who had run the New York City Marathon, and a seed was planted. During the next three years, driven by the suffering Terry saw around him in the cancer clinic, it sprouted. He would run across Canada. He trained and researched and planned. He would not be deterred.

Despite much initial skepticism, the sight of this young man hop-skipping 42 kilometres a day on an artificial leg would capture the hearts of Canadians all along his route and far beyond. On lonely roads, in punishing weather that could rattle and derail a car let alone a one-legged runner, Terry kept going, a marathon a day. Many wept as he ran awkwardly past. People waited hours to see him. The money began to trickle, then pour in.

Darrell Fox, then 17, joined his brother in Saint John, New Brunswick, and was with him to the end, a thrill he compares to riding a favourite amusement park ride—and never wanting to get off. "The best was seeing the impact he was having on people, the expressions of those watching as he ran by. It was one thing to know that Terry was running. It was another thing to actually see him run, the effort that it took."

On September 1, 1980, in Thunder Bay, Ontario, the ride came to a terrifying halt. Cancer had spread to Terry's lungs. An entire nation was shocked and saddened. By that point, Terry had raised $1.4 million, nowhere near his goal. But the Marathon of Hope was far from over. The day after Terry was forced off the road, Isadore Sharp, president of Four Seasons Hotels, vowed that a run would be held each year in Terry's name. Seven days later, a nationwide telethon by the CTV network brought in more than $10 million in just five hours.

In February 1981, Terry's dream came true. With the national population at 24.1 million, the Marathon of Hope fund reached $24.17 million. That he was no longer on the road didn't matter. Terry's enormous courage had touched hearts from coast to coast.

Terry Fox Marathon of Hope.

While he fought for his life, the honours mounted. He became the youngest Companion of the Order of Canada, the nation's top civilian honour. He was awarded the Order of the Dogwood, British Columbia's top civilian honour; the Sword of Hope, the highest honour bestowed by the American Cancer Society; the Lou Marsh Trophy for outstanding athletic achievement; and was named newsmaker of the year by Canadian Press. He won again in 1981, posthumously.

Terry died June 28, 1981, surrounded by his family. Across Canada, flags flew at half-mast. Canada's greatest hero—so declared in a national survey in 1999—was gone. But his accomplishments while he was alive only hinted at what he would accomplish in death. Terry's dream was just beginning.

On the first Terry Fox Run held that September, more than 300,000 people in 760 locations walked, ran, or cycled in his memory, raising $3.2 million. On the 20th anniversary run in 2000, more than 1.6 million people in 58 countries participated, raising $20.4

Terry Fox gives a speech at Toronto City Hall, Nathan Phillips Square, during a stop on his Marathon of Hope across Canada, July 11, 1980. (CP Photo/Bill Becker)

million. In 2001, $23 million was raised worldwide, $17 million in Canada. More than 4,200 elementary schools held their own individual runs with children born a generation after Terry's death.

"He would be most happy about how it's being raised, one dollar at a time," says Darrell. "That's what we got on the road. For the most part, that's what we're getting now. It was so important to Terry to keep it pure, without sponsorship, commercialism, or exploitation. We cherish and are so thankful for the loonies and toonies. That's what's adding up, not just large donations. The Terry Fox Run is a continuation of the Marathon of Hope."

Darrell talks about his big brother as only a little brother can. The awe can be heard in his voice. It's an awe shared by a nation, but is beyond words for the Fox family. "We're overwhelmed, just overwhelmed," says Betty Fox, who would look out the back of the van when on the road with Terry, too afraid to watch him run. "None of us thought about where it would go. We thought about his safety. We were proud but we were scared stiff. The feelings go so very deep. I'll never find the words. We deserve no credit. It belongs to Terry and those keeping his dream alive."

Darrell grieved for 10 years before he was ready to immerse himself in the dream again through the Terry Fox Foundation. "I never thought he would die. I thought he was invincible. To be able to say I'm Terry's brother is a real gift. I feel so fortunate. He's given so much to every member of our family because we were able to know him and witness what he has accomplished. To be a small part of his legacy is a gift. I will forever more shake my head when I look at what he did. He's my role model. He's my hero. His death proved to me that if cancer can take Terry Fox, then we have a fight on our hands."

I don't think this is unfair. That's the thing about cancer. I'm not the only one. It happens all the time, to other people. I'm not special. This just intensifies what I did. It gives it more meaning . . . I just wish people would realize that anything is possible if you try. Dreams are made if people try.

—TERRY FOX
(*Terry Fox: His Story*)

Terry Fox Foundation
National Office
789 Don Mills Road, Suite 802
Toronto, ON M3C 1T5
e-mail: national@terryfoxrun.org

Nancy Greene Raine
Inspiration to Generations

BORN: MAY 11, 1943
OTTAWA, ONTARIO

Sibling rivalry can be a wonderful thing. Just ask Nancy Greene Raine. The two-time world champion and Olympic gold-medallist alpine skier used to hit the slopes for fun. She had no intention of competing professionally, that is, until her sister started winning. "My ambition was to beat my sister Liz." With an incentive like that, it's no wonder she was nicknamed Tiger for being such a tough competitor.

Greene Raine learned to ski as she learned to walk. At age six, she conquered any fear of heights as her father tethered a rope around her waist and guided her down the steepest slopes of Red Mountain in Rossland, B.C. Years later, she conquered that same mountain as a world-class competitor.

At first, she skied for the pure enjoyment. Sister Elizabeth was the real competitor in those early years. Then, in 1958, the Canadian Junior Championships were held in her hometown of Rossland, and Liz was on the team. At 10 o'clock at night, the phone rang. It was the coach. A couple of the skiers had been injured. He knew 14-year-old Nancy skied, and wanted to know if she'd pinch-hit in the next day's competition. She did, and came third. Her

sister came first. The next day, Nancy came second. Her sister still came first. That's when the rivalry began.

Two years later, she was named an alternate for the 1960 Olympics in Squaw Valley, California. Right before the games, she won the U.S. National Championships, so officials decided to put the 16-year-old on the team. They didn't expect her to place, but they did hope it would give her some valuable experience.

Nancy's roommate at the games was Anne Heggtveit, Canada's best skier at the time. Nancy placed 26th. Heggtveit won gold. As Greene Raine watched her stand on the podium and Canada's national anthem filled the air, she resolved right there and then, that one day, she too would win gold.

Heggtveit was only the second Canadian woman to impress the international skiing circuit. In 1956, Lucille Wheeler won bronze at the Winter Olympics in Cortina D'Ampezzo. Greene Raine didn't know it at the time, but she was one of the first in a legacy of female alpine skiers who would all influence each other in some way. "If it wasn't for Nancy, I don't think people like Laurie Graham, Karen Percy, Kerrin Lee-Gartner—and Gerry Sorensen before

Skier Nancy Greene speeds down the hill in the first leg of the Women's Special Slalom at Chamrousse, Grenoble, France, during the 1968 Winter Olympics. Greene was voted the Female Athlete of the Century by Canadian radio news directors and newspaper editors in a poll conducted by the Canadian Press.

them—would have risen to prominence the way they did," the executive director of Canada's Sports Hall of Fame told the Canadian Press. "One feeds on the people that precede them," Allan Stewart said. "And they would all mention Nancy . . . What she did was set off a line of international success."

Despite her determination, Greene Raine didn't place in either the World Championships or Winter Olympics two years later. She attacked the slopes, skiing all out and crashing, or being too careful and too slow. She writes in her autobiography that her erratic results taught her the importance of control: "I learned that I could come up with better results and more consistent finishes if I held myself slightly in check, if I really concentrated on a course instead of almost blindly assaulting it."

Her breakthrough year came in 1965 when she consistently placed in the top

five and won four events in Europe. A "terrifically exciting" fall in the World Championships the next year made her even more determined to do better. She biked, ran, and even carried her brother to put him to bed as she strived to build her strength.

It paid off. In 1967, she took the lead in the first-ever World Cup circuit, returning to Canada in the middle of her winning streak to take part in international races held here. A lot of people criticized her for doing that. She missed three races and fell in the standings. "But I didn't consider remaining there for a minute," she says. Greene Raine wanted to give young skiers in Canada a taste of what high level competition was like, and her presence on the slopes provided a much-needed boost for ski programs. She then returned to the circuit and proved her critics wrong by taking the World Cup by 7/100ths of a second. Greene Raine was the best skier in the world. *Canadian Sport Monthly* called her accomplishment, "One of the greatest individual feats in amateur sports."

Greene Raine emerged from her competitions a more mature skier because, she says, she realized that there was more to life than winning, and so she relaxed and became more focused. She said 1967 was her most exciting and rewarding season because she trained with more determination and drive. But she thinks that she was also able to do so because skiing no longer defined her whole world. She was taking history at Notre Dame University in Nelson, B.C., and says doing well on her exams was important to her. It put racing into perspective: "I relaxed and, like magic, I found I could ski better, with more spirit and skill, than I had ever skied before."

She set her sights on gold at the 1968 Winter Olympics. "May the best win," rival Marielle Goitschel of France yelled at the start. And she did. Greene Raine won gold, the second Canadian to ever do so in Olympic history. In Vancouver, people took to the streets in green for her victory parade, and the city's newspapers were printed with green front pages.

Greene Raine ended where she began: on Red Mountain. She won the World Cup yet again on the very slopes she learned to ski on as a toddler. As the season wrapped up, Greene Raine realized she had accomplished everything she had set out to and retired at the top of her game, at age 24.

The skier didn't stop working, though. Named to the Order of Canada in 1968 for her contributions to sport, Greene Raine wrote books about her love of skiing. She also wrote an autobiography and delivered speeches about the determination and hard work it takes to make it in the sport, and in life in general. As well, Greene Raine developed an entry-level race program for children called the Nancy Greene Ski League. Thousands of children continue to hone their skills in the league every year.

Globe and Mail sports editor Jim Vipond wrote, in 1968: "Here is a young

Canada's women's alpine ski team—(from left) Ann Heggtveit (slalom gold-medal winner), Nancy Holland, Nancy Greene, and Elizabeth Greene—participated at the 1960 Squaw Valley Olympics.

woman who has become Canada's best unofficial diplomat; a young woman whose achievements as a skier have brought the name Canada to the fore in all countries where sport is a way of life." In 1999, Canadian Press named her Canada's female athlete of the century. "I'm absolutely thrilled and elated," she said after learning of the honour. " I'm surprised actually. I never really think of myself as being a super athlete."

Others do, however. Nancy Greene Raine's success helped make skiing popular in Canada at a time when it was receiving little government or public attention. Television was just beginning to make icons out of sports figures as Canadians watched Nancy Greene

Raine's success across Europe and North America. Canadian newspapers called her "Our Nancy," and she used that attention to generate money from corporations to develop the sport she loved.

It's been nearly 40 years since Nancy Greene Raine won Canadians' hearts, along with World and Olympic titles, but skiing remains her passion. To this day, there's nothing she loves more than to step into her boots, strap on her skis, and admire the pristine snow sparkling below her in the early morning light.

This athlete supports:
Nancy Greene Ski League
(various branches)

Rick Hansen
Still in Motion

BORN: AUGUST 26, 1957
PORT ALBERNI, BRITISH COLUMBIA

It was a warm early summer evening in June 1973. Fifteen-year-old Rick Hansen was bouncing along in the back of a pick-up truck with a buddy. They were hitchhiking home after a weekend fishing trip. Summer vacation had just begun—the long, lazy days ahead promised hours filled with what the two best friends loved to do—hunting, hiking, and camping. Seconds later, that carefree life was gone. As the driver pulled out of a long, slow curve, the truck went into a skid, flipping end over end and landing in a ditch. "There was a crunch. I distinctly remember hearing a crunch," Hansen writes in his autobiography, *Man in Motion*.

His back was broken and he was paralyzed from the waist down. (The other boy had only minor injuries and walked away from the accident.) But the young man who thought his dreams had broken that day went on to become an Olympian who would wheel around the world and help raise $100 million in his quest to find a cure for paralysis. He also married the love of his life, his physiotherapist, Amanda, and has three healthy daughters, "the most beautiful gift a person can be given."

Rick Hansen always dreamed of becoming an athlete. His accident just meant he had to take the hard road to get there. But he accomplished his dream, and as soon as he did, he set another goal and reached for it. Life hits you in waves, he says, but instead of feeling life has pulled one over on you, Hansen tells all kids—able bodied and disabled—"don't give up, redouble your efforts, work hard, and accept the help of others." He's living proof that if you do that, "anything's possible."

Doctors were brutally honest with Hansen after his injury. They told him he'd likely never walk again. But from that first day in hospital, he set goals for himself. Looking back on those times, he says, "One of the major things that saved me is that I focused on things I could do." First, he worked on his arms, building strength. His next goal was to be out of a special bed used by paralysis patients and into a normal hospital bed for his 16th birthday. Next, he mastered the wheelchair. Once he did that, he set his sights on being home to graduate with his friends. He accomplished all that, and so much more.

He constantly pushed himself in rehab. One day, braces strapped around his immobile legs, Hansen pulled himself up at the parallel bars and, for the first time in months, stood on his own two

Canada's Mel Fitzgerald (left) and Rick Hansen compete in the wheelchair event at the 1984 Olympic Games in Los Angeles.

feet. His arms shook terribly, but, he says, "To me it was the victory stand at the Olympics, and I'd just won the gold."

He was out of the rehabilitation centre in three months—half the time it was expected to take. After graduating from high school, Hansen applied to the physical education program at the University of British Columbia. Without giving a concrete reason for not accepting him, the admissions department suggested he apply to the arts department, saying it would consider him for the physical education program in his second year. Hansen was accepted that second year and mastered wheelchair sports in a way no one had before him. He became not only known as the best wheelchair athlete in the world but also the first person with a disability to earn a physical education degree in Canada. Hansen says it's another example of his determination to change attitudes and perceptions about the potential of people with disabilities, and he's proud he set a precedent.

Hansen took the pressures of adversity and transformed them into accomplishments, doing things most—even

29

those who can walk—would never consider. There were, of course, times he was filled with fear and uncertainty when looking at what lay ahead, but he met each challenge head on. "I felt an expression of myself was gone," Hansen recalls about his learning he was paralyzed. He thought he'd spend his life confined to an institution or his home. "But I was limited by knowledge rather than my disability," he says.

There were also times he felt sorry for himself; like when he headed down to the lake with his friends. Instead of going swimming like he used to, he'd sit in the pick-up truck and sulk. "My view of independence and wholeness was to do everything myself." But he soon learned to accept the help of friends and mentors: "My disability wasn't a disability, my attitude to it was. All I had to do was ask for help, reach out, and I soon saw the folly of my views."

Hansen says he had some fantastic role models to help him along the way. "Everybody has a chance to have heroes or role models in life, and you don't need to go to TV or books. They're in everyday lives, in our families, communities." One of his greatest heroes is his dad. A worker for the local phone company, he broke his hip when a telephone

pole he was working at the top of fell. Like his son, Hansen senior was athletic at the time and ended up suffering a serious disability and severe pain. But, says son Rick, "He never complained. If he wanted to do something, he just went out and did it."

Stan Stronge was another of Rick's heroes. He became a paraplegic in 1938 and spent four years in the hospital. In those days before antibiotics, he was never expected to pull through. But he did, and later pushed Rick into competitive wheelchair sports. "He decided he was going to live, and he lived a quality life," Hansen says. Stronge devoted himself to the disabled and wheelchair sports through the Canadian Paraplegic Association and other wheelchair sporting organizations. "He came along and challenged me, and gave me a sense of what's possible," says Hansen.

In the next few years, Hansen competed in marathons around the globe, becoming the best wheelchair athlete in the world. He shared Canada's Outstanding Male Athlete of the Year Award with hockey great Wayne Gretzky in 1983. And on May 22, 1987, he completed the odyssey that saw him named a Companion of the Order of Canada for his commitment to others.

Christopher Reeve (left) and Rick Hansen (right) at the Toronto General Hospital for "The Spark of Life" campaign, 1996.

Two years, two months, and two days after he left home on the Man in Motion World Tour, Hansen rolled into Vancouver after wheeling the circumference of the world.

More than 40,000 kilometres. That's 94 pairs of worn out gloves, 126 flat tires, 30,000 pushes of the wheel every day. He pushed his wheelchair up mountains so steep, it would roll back when he took his hands off the wheel; pain wracked his elbows, back, and wrists; driving snow cut into his face; he bowed his head to the beating rain and merciless sun. There were times public support touched his soul—like when the poor Portuguese villagers pressed their meagre offerings into his hand. Others were apathetic, driving by in their luxury cars without giving a penny.

But Hansen said his greatest challenge was in his own head: "self-doubt, skepticism, cynicism"—these are what threatened to keep him from his goal. And "constantly worrying about what could go wrong." But he was so committed to his cause, he forced himself to put all that

31

aside to focus on the task at hand. His aim was to raise awareness about spinal cord injuries, and money to do research. So, instead of letting his fears consume him, he surrounded himself with good people, trained relentlessly, and took each day moment by moment, stroke by stroke.

He set a goal of $10 million. He raised $24 million. Through ongoing funds, programs, and organizations, Rick Hansen has so far contributed more than $100 million to spinal cord injury education, research, and rehabilitation, and to wheelchair sports. "That journey transformed my life. I set one new goal and one big dream after another. Now my dream is to find a cure for spinal cord injury . . . Our organization (the Rick Hansen Institute) is totally focused to push that forward."

But Hansen still has time for a few other causes close to his heart. He has created a program to promote postsecondary education for students with disabilities. And he has never put aside his passion for fishing and the environment. He's currently trying to restore sturgeon stocks in the Fraser River as chair of the Fraser River Sturgeon Conservation Society.

When that pick-up truck flipped over and severed Rick Hansen's spinal cord nearly 30 years ago, he was devastated. He thought his life was over. His life was filled with physical pain and emotional anguish. But if he could go back to that moment, he says he wouldn't change it. Life has been difficult, but it has allowed him to become a stronger person. He says he's richer for the challenges life has presented him.

"At the time, I thought it was the worst thing that could happen. Now, I think it's the best thing. I'd never trade the life I have today for the life I could have had; there's just no way. Success is not measured by whether you use your legs or not—it's how you live your life."

This athlete supports:
Rick Hansen Institute
University of British Columbia
1874 East Mall, Room 1040
Vancouver, BC V6T 1Z1

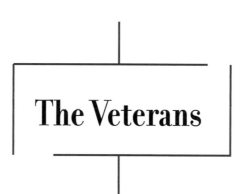

The Veterans

Elvis Stojko
Undaunted by Challenges

BORN: MARCH 22, 1972
NEWMARKET, ONTARIO

His muscular body is crunched over in pain. Hands clasped over his knees, agony is written all over Elvis Stojko's face. This was, yet again, another painful challenge to the world-class figure skater's career.

It was January 1995. The Olympic silver medallist had just won Skate Canada and the Nations Cup. He was practising for the Canadian Championships at the Metro Centre in Halifax when he slammed into the boards, tearing a ligament in his ankle. It hurt, but he had worked too long and too hard to give up. It wasn't in his nature.

Looking back, Stojko says he just had to try to defend the title he had taken from Kurt Browning the year before. "I had worked so hard for the title, I had to give it everything I had." If he didn't at least try, he knew it would bother him for the rest of his life. To the amazement of figure skating fans across the country, Stojko did lace up his skates and glide out onto the ice. Soon, though, it was obvious he couldn't continue. He was disappointed, but satisfied he had given it everything he had.

That moment, perhaps more than any other, summarizes Elvis Stojko's character. Always do your best, and try your hardest. Pursue excellence. Every-

one makes mistakes, he says, but the important thing is to learn from them. "Never let anyone take away your dreams," he urges up-and-coming skaters and kids he visits in schools. "You have one life to live, one shot at it, so give it everything you've got."

It's that strength of character and determination that put him on the gold-medal podium at the world championships just weeks after his injury in Halifax. It was an accomplishment Stojko rates as one of the highlights of his career. Instead of bemoaning his bad luck, he used the accident to focus on the Worlds. He started retraining an hour at a time, then a day at a time, gradually working up to his full training schedule. But just two weeks before the competition, he couldn't yet land a triple jump.

Undaunted, he took the title by not only opening his program with a triple axel/triple toe combination but by ending with a spectacular triple/triple. When it was over, he waved proudly to the crowd. Once again, he had made a triumphant comeback. Stojko says it is those kinds of challenges that helped sculpt the person he is today. "Don't allow your difficulties to hold you back," he advises. "Don't get discouraged

Canadian skater Elvis Stojko performs in the men's free program of the Four Continents Figure Skating Championships in Osaka, Japan, February 27, 2000. Stojko won the championship.

injury and had trouble focusing when a personal relationship went sour.

"It was a true test for all my philosophies in life," Stojko says, reflecting on the dark time. "All my belief systems were shattered. Everything I believed in myself was gone. I had to pick up the pieces physically, mentally, one step at a time." It was like being in a dark room, he says, filled with puzzle pieces, but being unable to figure out how they go together. Eventually though, with the support and advice of friends, family, and his coach, he pulled it together and took the silver medal at the 1998 Winter Olympics in Nagano, Japan.

Stojko has never taken the easy route in his career or his life. He has set his own course, determined to be true to his personal beliefs, rather than bending to what the public—or the judges— might call for. At times, it cost him. In 1992, he was a medal hopeful for the 1992 Winter Olympics in Albertville. He had a stylish program filled with karate moves taken from the sport he loves, but it was different from what the judges were used to seeing. He knew the

or look for excuses or reasons to fail." You can't control everything that happens to you, but you can control the way you respond.

Stojko won the World Championships in 1994 and 1995, but fell in 1996, prompting some commentators to suggest he was all washed-up. Those critics were left red-faced as he regained the title in 1997 when he landed the first-ever quad-triple in competition. In 1998, the naysayers jumped on him again when he suffered a severe groin figure-skating world might not be ready for it, but he took it to the ice anyway. The crowd went wild, but the judges were less kind. Stojko finished seventh.

"A judge will never, ever take away my confidence or take control of me," Stojko said at the time. "I am who I am, and who I want to be. I'll never change myself just to win a gold medal." In the end, he hasn't needed to. Judges have come to appreciate Stojko's style, earning him an unprecedented six gold medals in Canadian competition and giving him 14 first-place finishes internationally.

Stojko retired after placing a disappointing eighth at the 2002 Winter Olympics in Salt Lake City, Utah. He realized his competitive skating days were over and so turned professional. When a reporter asked Stojko what he wanted other skaters to remember him for, he replied, "That I've made a difference. I wasn't someone who just won and walked away."

Stojko never did get that elusive Olympic gold, but he has another medal hanging around his neck that's just as valuable. It was given to him by his aunt and uncle when the judging controversy placed him second in Albertville. Engraved on it are the words "Sixteenth

Olympic Winter Games" along with the Olympic rings. On the back, it says, "Congratulations, Elvis. You're Number One." They were telling him that he was their champion. "It was very sentimental," he says.

Stojko's success comes as no surprise to his mother Irene. Watching Elvis on the ice when he was just five—skating in a pair of white girl's skates she'd bought and painted black she knew he had promise. She watched him train hard to hone and focus his talent, often doing his homework in the car between practices. She watched over the years as he developed his own unique, captivating style of skating, often combining martial arts or even rock music with technical mastery.

Figure-skating icon Brian Orser says Elvis was never one to mimic other skaters. He created a style all his own through years of steadily progressing up the ladder. Even when he did mimic others for fun—such as the Jailhouse Rock number he did for his parents, who had named him after their favourite rock 'n' roll singer—he added his own touch. Stojko studied Presley's hip gyrations and incorporated them into his program, all the while retaining his own personality.

Three-time world figure skating champion Elvis Stojko instructs young skaters, including Holly Smith (front left), from Hastings, Ontario, at a clinic in Brampton, Ontario, 1999.

In 1991, Stojko was the first to land a quadruple/double jump combination in competition. Six years later, he became the first ever to land a quadruple/triple jump combination in competition. He achieved them through sheer hard work and sacrifice.

Stojko's life isn't all skating. He also shares his dreams of determination with children as ambassador for Ronald McDonald House Charities, working with children with life-threatening or chronic illnesses and disabilities. He recalls being touched deeply by one 12-year-old girl. She had done a television commercial with him while her cancer was in remission. But the cancer came back. Stojko went to her home and met with her for a couple of hours. "It was just us; we just chatted." He told her that as her strength waned, the sun was getting brighter because of all the lives she had touched. She had such a short life, "but her purpose was to lift people up by her courage." She led a difficult life, "but a very fulfilling life. She was a very happy kid with amazing support, and she touched the lives of so many people. She was very special. You get touched by it. You look at the person, not the situation."

Stojko, too, has done so much with his life and has touched so many people. So what's next? Believe it or not, Hollywood: "My big, big, big dream is to be in a *Star Wars* movie." He's got all the action figures and winged fighters. And doesn't care if he's unrecognizable, garbed in gruesome disguise—he just wants to be in the movie. And as with everything in life, he's going to, he says, just "jump right in and work my butt off."

This athlete supports:
Ronald McDonald Children's
Charities of Canada
McDonald's Place
Toronto, ON M3D 3L4
e-mail: rmcc@mcdonalds.ca

Sandra Schmirler
Queen of Curling

BORN: JUNE 11, 1963
BIGGAR, SASKATCHEWAN
DIED MARCH 2, 2000, AT AGE 36

She was the queen of curling who won the hearts of Canadians for her amazing victories on the ice, and for that one tragic battle she lost off it. Sandra Schmirler, one of Canada's most accomplished athletes, was the greatest skip in the history of Canadian women's curling, having won three national and world titles and the gold medal at the 1998 Olympics in Nagano, Japan.

But Schmirler's story is about much more than winning. Her story is that of a fierce competitor who curled because it was fun. It's about motherhood, family, and friends, which were more important than anything to her. It's about an elite athlete and a star who, in her unassuming way, chatted with fans on the street and in the grocery store. And it's about the tenacious spirit and courage of an engaging personality who was a role model for women, for curling, for athletes, and for the ordinary Canadian.

Schmirler died of cancer on March 2, 2000, at age 36. She left behind husband, Shannon England, two young daughters—Sara, who was two and a half when her mother died, and Jenna, nine months—three teammates who were also her closest friends, and legions of fans, about 12,000 of whom gathered for her funeral in Regina, Saskatchewan, where flags on all provincial buildings flew at half mast. The rest of the country watched on television. In a rare tribute, Schmirler's funeral was broadcast nationwide.

"She was a simple prairie girl who brought the country together, and she did it extremely well," says Dave Parkes, chief executive officer of the Canadian Curling Association, who travelled with Schmirler's team for national and international competitions and became a close friend. "Winning didn't change who she was and what she was all about. It's a great lesson for anyone. Her legacy will be a part of curling always, but it transcends curling. She showed us so many things. She showed us that to be successful, things had to be kept in perspective. It was only a game. She kept her sporting life rooted in reality. She was first and foremost a great friend to teammates. She was a fierce competitor, but sport came second to family."

For more than anyone, Schmirler left a legacy for women in sport, adds Parkes. "Sandra and her team were athletes, yet all were wives and mothers who also had careers. She showed us how to keep life in a balance. She showed us that having fun is an integral part of success. She played to win every game and tried to make every shot count, but fun was a key component of the team's approach."

In the years since her death, Schmirler's impact has only grown stronger. It promises to endure and inspire indefinitely, joining the legacy of such great Canadians as Terry Fox. The Sandra Schmirler Foundation, established after her death by the Canadian Curling Association and Scott Paper Ltd., easily generated $150,000 in just nine months following her death. In 2001, that total exceeded $250,000. The foundation, which honours Schmirler's achievements and her love of family, children, and sport, helps families with children challenged by life-threatening illness. In 2001, the foundation made its first donation—$75,000 to be shared by the Ronald McDonald House, Cystic Fibrosis Foundation, and the Children's Miracle Network.

But as big as Schmirler became and remains, she was part of a package, and she made sure people knew it. She was a team member, one of four great women similar in skill, age, and stage of life, who would come off the ice to breast-feed their babies and jump back on to win.

Women across Canada were drawn to the team. "We found as we became successful and out in the public eye that women just kind of flocked to us because they felt we were one of them," says teammate Joan McCusker. "We didn't have the perfect body types, we

Team Canada skip Sandra Schmirler delivers her rock during ninth draw competition against Quebec at the Canadian Women's Curling Championships in Regina. Canada beat Quebec 9–3 and had a record of four wins and two losses.

weren't very young. We were women with careers and husbands and children. Still, we were competitive and had goals, and we helped each other achieve them."

One reason for the team's success and longevity, adds McCusker, was Schmirler's respect for her teammates in a sport where the skip usually gets the credit and attention. "Sandra always shared the spotlight. She continually tried to divert the limelight to the rest of us. She really showed curlers how to act in this regard," says McCusker. "It endeared her to many people."

Schmirler was born the youngest of three daughters of Art and Shirley Schmirler. Growing up, she excelled both academically and athletically, participating in swimming, volleyball, fastball, badminton, and track. It was curling, however, which she started playing at age 12, that emerged as her favourite sport. In high school, she would play on two provincial championship teams.

She went on to study physical education at the University of Saskatchewan in Saskatoon, before moving to Regina. There, she curled as a third on a team with Jan Betker, who would become a close friend and life-long curling partner. After a disappointing performance at

the 1990 provincial championships, Schmirler decided to form her own team. In addition to Betker as third, she recruited Marcia Gudereit as lead and Joan McCusker as second.

This team would go on to win six provincial championships, three Canadian championships (in 1993, 1994, and 1997), the World Championships in the same years, and the 1998 Olympic gold in Japan. Its success was unprecedented. No women's team consisting of the same four members had ever won more than one world title. The Olympic gold, meanwhile, was the first-ever Olympic medal in curling, since it was the sport's inaugural appearance at the games.

The excitement the team generated brought them the title of Team of the Year in 1998 by Canadian Press, and landed them in the Canadian Curling Hall of Fame in 1999, and in Canada's Sports Hall of Fame in 2000.

But the team's greatest accomplishment wasn't the Olympic gold medal— at least not to the team. It was simply getting to the games. In the year leading up to the Olympic trials, all the women had had babies. Schmirler, who was pregnant at the 1997 World Curling Championships, had a 2-month-old baby (Sara) by the time the Olympic

Children play in the Sandra Schmirler Olympic Gold Park in Biggar, Saskatchewan, August 7, 2000, while inside the school gymnasium, dignitaries, family members, and friends of the late Canadian curling champion gather to officially open the park. About 1,200 people were on hand for the opening, including Deputy Prime Minister Herb Gray. Schmirler's husband, Shannon England, told the crowd he would make sure their two young children would make frequent visits to Biggar from their home in Regina to visit "mom's park."

trials came along. McCusker had a 5-year-old youngster and a 1-year-old infant. Betker had a 1-year-old, and Gudereit had an 11-month-old. "There we were trying to get back into shape and we won the provincial, the Canadian, and the World's," says McCusker with a laugh. "We would curl, go breast-feed, pump breast milk, do whatever it took, then get back out

there. I look back and shake my head."

Competitiveness in women, adds McCusker, is often seen as a negative. "Sandra was someone who showed that it's okay to channel that competitiveness into a sport, especially a sport that women can have a career in for a long period of time. We were proud to represent that kind of image to all women out there."

45

As Schmirler's profile grows with her legacy, McCusker sometimes wonders if Schmirler the Curler would be happy about that. What made Schmirler so special was how ordinary she remained despite all the attention. "She was very much the girl next door and she worked hard to maintain that," says McCusker.

Yet for Sara and Jenna, who are being raised by dad Shannon England with the help of Schmirler's mom, Shirley, McCusker is glad Schmirler's star is shining so brightly. "I'm happy that it's happening for her two young daughters, who didn't get to know her. I'm happy there's a legacy out there that they can look up to, a way for them to get to know their mom."

As for the team, they're still hanging out, still playing, still competing. Betker has taken over as skip and there's a new player, Sherry Linton. They are ranked number two on the women's bonspiel tour. As always, they're shooting for number one.

Sandra Schmirler Foundation

1660 Vimont Court

Cumberland, ON K4A 4J4

George Chuvalo
Fighting to Make a Difference

BORN: SEPTEMBER 12, 1937
TORONTO, ONTARIO

During two decades as Canada's top heavyweight boxer, George Chuvalo traded punches with the best fighters of the last century. He went toe-to-toe with legends such as George Foreman, Joe Frazier, and Floyd Patterson. He fought Muhammad Ali twice, and though he didn't win either time, he was the first boxer to ever go 15 rounds against him. But as he straddles a chair at the front of a school gymnasium, telling his life story to 170 children too young to know about his bone-crushing battles in the ring, it's clear the most punishing blows of his life have come outside it.

In the decade that followed his retirement in 1979, life for the Toronto-born Canadian Sports Hall of Famer spiralled into a "hell on earth" that culminated with the loss of three of his sons and his wife to drug abuse. But drawing on the same inner strength that kept him on his feet during all of his 97 career fights, Chuvalo emerged from the heartache with a mission: To make sure other families don't have to feel his kind of pain. Since 1996, he has travelled to more than 500 schools and spoken in numerous detention centres in an unrelenting one-man war to deglamourize drugs. "Recalling what happened to my family because of drugs is tougher than anything that happened to me in the ring," he says. "I don't mince words; I don't preach. I tell it like it is. I've seen what happens close up and it's not pretty."

Chuvalo isn't sure how his sons' drug problems started. Maybe it was the pressure of having a heavyweight champion for a dad. Maybe they were genetically predisposed to being addicts, he says. Whatever the reason, by 1984, it was clear three of them were heavily into drugs. "None of my sons could beat heroin," he tells the students. "They were pathetic, pitiful. It hurts me to speak of my sons this way, but I have to. I have to let you know how awful drugs really are."

Jesse, Chuvalo's youngest son, got into cocaine while recuperating from a motorcycle accident. He took a friend's advice and tried it at a party as a way to ease the pain. A year later, on February 18, 1985, he went into his bedroom and shot himself. He was 20.

Jesse's older brothers, George Lee and Steven, were into heroin. They were in and out of jail as they repeatedly turned to crime to feed their habits. In one robbery, the pair used a butcher knife and a hatchet to demand drugs from a chemist. Even as police chased after them in the street, Chuvalo says, they "stuffed handfuls of pills into their mouths like mad dogs, using only their saliva to swallow them."

George Lee died of a heroin overdose in 1993, just four weeks after being released from prison. It was all too much for Chuvalo's wife, Lynne. She died of an overdose of prescription drugs four days later.

Chuvalo had met Lynne in 1957, one year after he stepped into the ring for the first time. It was a heavyweight novice tournament, and he knocked out four opponents in a total of 13 minutes and 36 seconds to collect his first paycheque: $500. Lynne was 13 years old when they met, and Chuvalo was almost 20. They dated for two years, and married when she was 15. By the time she was 20, they had four children: Mitchell,

Canadian heavyweight champion George Chuvalo fighting world heavyweight champion Muhammad Ali at Maple Leaf Gardens, March 29, 1966. Ali won the match after 15 rounds. (CP Photo/Boris Spremo, C.M.)

Steven, George Lee, and Jesse. The couple's last child, Vanessa, was born three years later.

There was turmoil in the relationship as money flowed freely following wins and dried up after losses, as well as during the early, aimless years of retirement. But unquestionably, Chuvalo loved Lynne. Her death was a body blow that almost toppled him. But the pain didn't end with her death. Drugs gradually sucked the life out of Steven too. He was so addicted to heroin, he would "crap his pants" at the sight of the drug, says Chuvalo. He overdosed 15 times in a two-month period and disappeared for days, only to be found passed out, nearly naked, in a snow bank with pill bottles in his hand.

Chuvalo details Steven's demise graphically to counter the glamourous images Hollywood sometimes uses when it portrays the drug culture. Although he's appeared in a three films himself—*The Fly, Prom Night Three,* and *The Untouchables*—Chuvalo swears he'd never do a film like *Pulp Fiction,* in which John Travolta's character, a gangster and heroin user, comes off as hip and sexy. "There's nothing hip about having your stomach pumped or listening to a user squeal for his next fix, or

watching a healthy body melt down and waste away. In real life, the Travolta character would be mangy looking; he'd look emaciated; he'd be in pain."

Chuvalo starts each of his presentations with a 1995 CBC *Fifth Estate* documentary about his family's fight with drugs. When it comes to the part where Steven talks earnestly from a jail cell about getting out, going straight, and going on the road with his dad to talk about the evils of drugs, Chuvalo weeps.

Steven never made it. Eleven days after being let out of jail in August 1996, he died of a heroin overdose at his sister Vanessa's house. "The police found him in his underwear, with a syringe sticking out of his arm and a cigarette in between his fingers," his father says. "It worked so fast, he was dead before he had a chance to light the cigarette."

Chuvalo isn't afraid to stray beyond the theme of drugs in his talks. He criticizes smoking, encourages a healthy lifestyle, and freely offers up his belief that love helps people deal with adversity: It gives young people the strength to make the right choices in the face of peer pressure. If you have love in your life, you have a chance to stand on your feet, he says. How could you expect a young person who is at the crossroads of

Mitch Chuvalo, son of former Canadian heavyweight boxer George Chuvalo, holds up a football in Toronto, November 29, 2000 after being named High School Football Coach of the Year for all of Canada. Chuvalo, who coaches at Western Technical Commercial High School in Toronto, was selected from a shortlist of 10 candidates. (CP Photo/Toronto Star—Colin McConnell)

his or her life to make sound decisions without love?

His daughter Vanessa steered clear of the drug scene and has been in the restaurant trade since graduating from university. In June 2001, she opened a small but trendy restaurant in Toronto called C'est Cheese and hopes to expand the operation as business grows. She's witnessed her father's anti-drug presentations a couple of times. They stir up disturbing memories for her, but she said they hit home with audiences and have a therapeutic effect on her

father. In addition to his own tours, Chuvalo makes appearances for the United Food and Commercial Workers Union, the Children's Wish Foundation, and the Salvation Army.

There are few mementos of Chuvalo's life as a boxer in the modest apartment he shares with his second wife, Joanne, and her two children. There's an oversize fight poster at the front door showing him clobbering Floyd Patterson in a 1965 Madison Square Garden match and a scrap book on a side table, but little else.

More visible—and more important to him—are the mementos of his fight against drugs. There are plaques and drawings and letters of appreciation from schools; hundreds of coffee cups emblazoned with high school crests; a copy of the anti-drug video he did with the Montreal arts community; and the medal he received when he was inducted into the Order of Canada in 1996 for his service to children.

On his desk, not far from a note from his wife suggesting changes to the Fight Against Drugs website that he operates to reach kids he can't see in person, there's a letter from a woman in Barrie, Ontario, that he treasures. In neat script, the woman tells him how her teenage son had come home from one of his presentations and told her that he loved her. It was the first time he'd said that to her in years. "The light went on for him. He realized the importance of family. That's the kind of thing that makes me want to keep on doing what I'm doing for years," says Chuvalo.

At 64, he's a little beefier than in his fighting days, but he still works out three times a week and can bench-press 400 pounds. He spends a lot of time with his family and loves to watch football games coached by another Chuvalo: his son Mitch teaches physical education at Western Technical Commercial High School in Toronto and was named High School Coach of the Year for the 1999-2000 season by the CFL and NFL International. "I'm thrilled for him," says the senior Chuvalo. "He's making a big difference in young people's lives."

This athlete supports:
Fight Against Drugs
18 Lagos Road
Etobicoke, ON M9W 4E4
website: www.fightagainstdrugs.ca

Paul Henderson
Making Life Count

BORN: JANUARY 28, 1943
LUCKNOW, ONTARIO

It's known simply as The Goal. It will always be The Goal. It's been 30 years and still most Canadians can recall exactly where they were when Paul Henderson made the most famous shot on net in Canadian history.

It was September 28, 1972, the eighth and final game of the Summit Series, pitting the two superpowers of hockey—Canada and the Soviet Union—against each other. Canada trailed from the start of the game but, incredibly, in the final seconds, the team had a chance to win. With 34 seconds on the clock, Henderson gave Canada a 6–5 win to clinch the series and ignite a joyous frenzy across Canada.

"Henderson has scored for Canada," cried announcer Foster Hewitt, recording the magical moment, considered one of the most significant in the country's sporting history. Henderson's life would never be the same. That single hockey point would turn him into a national hero and cause the team to be named Canada's Team of the Century. The moment would rank eighth among most significant events of the last 100 years in Canadian history, just behind such epic events as Confederation, the 1917 battle for Vimy Ridge, and the Normandy landing on D-Day in June 1944.

And it would eventually launch Henderson on a spiritual journey that would bring him to a very different place in life, one just as fulfilling as hockey but with goals that have little to do with shooting a puck, success that has nothing to do with money, and winning that is not about competition.

Henderson is a coach these days, but not on the ice. He still excites a crowd, but the arena has changed. Since 1984, he's been ministering to men about priorities, about keeping a balance in life, about leaving a legacy of which they can be proud. President and CEO of The Leadership Group, Henderson is using his profile to encourage and challenge men to look at the spiritual dimension of their lives and the kind of people they are as husbands, fathers, grandfathers, brothers, sons, and friends. The purpose of his organization is "to impact belief, character, and action" through men's groups—there are now about 70 in Southern Ontario—where men can go for encouragement, guidance, prayer, and sharing.

Henderson embraced Christianity in 1975. His gifts now are encouragement and exhortation. He has about 100 speaking engagements a year across the country. He also leads weekend marriage conferences with wife Eleanor, with whom he has been married 39 years and has raised three daughters. And he supports various community groups and charities, such as the Special Olympics, Muskoka Woods Sports Camp and Teen Ranch, the organ donation program at the Hospital for Sick Children, and various missions.

"As a kid growing up, I just wanted to have the good life. I wanted to be successful and financially independent. I wanted a job that I really enjoyed. My first choice was to be a NHL player, something I was able to attain. I wanted to share my life with a woman I could love. I wanted the home, the car, the country club. Then '72 came along and I had those things, and I was the toast of Canada, so I had some notoriety also.

"But when I was really honest about it, there was a lot of worry in my life, a

Members of Team Canada 1972, Toronto, October 10, 2000, inspecting original memorabilia donated to the Hockey Hall of Fame on the occasion of the Canadian Press naming the team the Team of the Century. From left: Ron Ellis, Paul Henderson, memorabilia donor Gary Smith, Rod Seiling, and Ken Dryden.

lot of fears, a lot of bitterness, a lot of anger. Someone encouraged me to look at the spiritual dimension of life, something I had never done. It was through the frustration of having everything I thought I needed and not being content that brought me here. There was hollowness inside, a lack of quietness or contentment. I didn't know how to deal with it, until I found Christianity. It changed me from the inside out."

Henderson's message? Make life count. "We're only going through here once, so slow down. Ask yourself what's really important. Life is a challenge every day. It's a challenge being a good husband. It's a challenge raising children. Developing and maintaining good relationships and friendships take time and effort. And if you sacrifice these things on the altar of materialism and career, you end up at the end of the day a pretty hollow person," he says. Henderson understands the reticence of many men to look inside themselves: "I identify with them because I know their fears. We were taught to suck it up. Never show weakness. That's the worst definition of what a man should be."

Almost every day, people still thank Henderson for scoring hockey's most memorable goal on that fall day, when schools were let out, when strangers hugged each other in joy, when patriotism soared. There could be no greater pinnacle of a hockey career that saw Henderson play 13 seasons with Detroit and Toronto in the NHL, and five seasons in the World Hockey Association. He also represented Canada against the Soviets during the 1974–5 season.

Henderson grew up in Lucknow, Ontario, having entered the world in another moment of drama. He was born January 28, 1943, on a horse-drawn sleigh in a snowstorm while his mother, Evelyn, tried to reach a hospital. His father, Garnet Henderson, was station agent for the Canadian National Railway who demanded a lot from his athletic son. Like so many Canadian boys at that time, Henderson's skating days began on a pond playing with friends.

On teams, Henderson was often placed with older boys. In a small town with not enough players to fill the various levels of hockey—bantam, midget, and juvenile—Henderson would play in more than one level in a season. He first caught the eye of scouts at age 15, and at 16 he joined the junior team of the Detroit Red Wings—the Hamilton Red Wings. After winning the Memorial Cup in 1962, he moved to the NHL.

Paul Henderson warms up before a charity game with past Team Canada players at Maple Leaf Gardens in Toronto. This weekend marked the 25th anniversary of their 1972 Canada–USSR Summit Series in which Henderson's goal in the final 34 seconds of the eighth and final game won the series.

It was a career of many highs, although no moment as famous as The Goal. He led the Ontario Hockey Association in goals in the regular season in 1963, played in two Stanley Cup finals for Detroit in 1964 and 1966, played in two NHL all-star games in 1972 and 1973, recorded 4 30-goal seasons, including two in the NHL, and 12 20-goal seasons, including 7 in the NHL.

Before retiring in 1981, he would amass 1,228 pro games, 388 goals, and 399 assists.

But it was the 1972 series that forever defined Henderson for Canadians.

In addition to that incredible moment at the 34-second mark in the final game, Henderson also scored the winning goals in games six and seven. His achievements landed him in the Canadian Sports Hall of Fame and on a commemorative coin minted in 1997 which depicts the winning goal. He can also be found on a Canada Post stamp celebrating the historic moment.

In November 2000, the Hockey Hall of Fame honoured Henderson, but not in the traditional way. A monument located in front of the Hall has been dedicated to Team Canada 1972. It depicts Henderson being hugged by teammate Yvon Cournoyer in the seconds after the game eight winning goal.

If he could live his life over, Henderson says he wouldn't change a thing, except perhaps that he would have become a Christian earlier. "I loved being a hockey player. I love what I do now. I would like to do this until the day I die. Hockey definitely brought me here. I've scored all the goals I'll ever need; now it's about what I leave behind. I don't think about being a role model for hockey. It's far more important for me to be a role model as a husband, father, and grandfather."

This athlete supports:
Teen Ranch
Christian Sports Camp
Box 77
Caledon, ON L0N 1C0
e-mail: info@teenranch.on.ca

BORN: NOVEMBER 14, 1964
MISSISSAUGA, ONTARIO

Silken Laumann eased herself down into the shell of her small boat. It was a warm, sunny day on still waters, and Canada's new hero was ready to row for her country in the 1992 Olympic Games in Barcelona.

With just 250 metres remaining in the single sculls final, U.S. silver-medallist Anne Marden rowed past Laumann into third place. Laumann, with not a thought for her bandaged leg, responded by digging deeper and harder, increasing her pace by two strokes a minute in the last 100 metres. Her muscles screamed from the effort, but she edged out Marden at the finish line.

That precious moment was the greatest victory of Laumann's life. She didn't win gold—she won bronze. But she had a far greater victory. "Quite simply it was a best effort given the circumstances," she says. Her coach, Mike Spracklen, said moments after the race, "Winning isn't always about finishing first, is it? Sometimes it's about conquering yourself."

Just 12 weeks earlier, the scull of a German pair's boat cut across Laumann's path during warm-ups for a regatta in Germany. The pointed bow ripped into her lower right leg, shredding it. She later told a reporter for the *Toronto Sun*,

"I looked at the leg for a few seconds and knew it was serious when my muscle was hanging at my ankle and I could see the bone."

Her leg was shattered, as were her dreams of Olympic gold. But rather than wallow in sorrow, Laumann used it to focus on what she wanted in life— and that was to be one of the world's best rowers. Doctors told her that her professional and maybe even recreational rowing life was over. She was crushed but didn't lose focus. In fact, while she was being taken by ambulance to a trauma centre just hours after the accident, she told her boyfriend at the time, Canadian rower John Wallace, she would compete in the Olympics. She even did exercises in her hospital bed to keep herself in shape. Less than a month after the accident, Wallace, whom she eventually married, helped her from her wheelchair and into her shell. And she began training for the Olympics.

She still walked with a cane by the time the Olympic torch was lit, but that didn't stop her from rowing. To compete took courage, but winning bronze showed her iron determination. It was the professional highlight of Laumann's rowing career. Looking back on that

Silken Laumann, bronze medal winner in the single sculls rowing event at the 1992 Barcelona Olympic Games.

day, Laumann told Judy Hasday, author of *Extraordinary Women Athletes,* that, "I chose to work on the premise that there was a little light at the end of the tunnel, and that I could work towards that light." Anne Marden, who came fourth in the race that day, told *Sports Illustrated* after the race, "I'll be devastated about that race for the rest of my life."

Laumann doesn't row competitively anymore but says she wants to take her message to young people everywhere that sheer force of will can get you what you want in life. She travels to schools in her home province of B.C., often carrying with her one of her medals in a briefcase. "I hope through public speaking to give young girls and boys a sense of what it's really like. The guts, the glory, the self-doubt, the worry. I talk about the times I wanted to quit, and that you have to recognize that your performance is in your own hands. I want to give them some encouragement, to tell them it's okay to fail. It's okay not to be first."

Friendly words of encouragement worked for her when she was down. And she wants to be able to tell kids that she's seen rough times, too, both in her personal life when her parents split up and as an athlete. But she pulled through, and she wants the kids to know that, whether their challenges are in sport or everyday life, they can make it too. "I had to overcome fear, push through that fear and my own self doubts," says Laumann. There were days she just wanted to give up and live a normal life. But she encourages youth to just take life one day at a time, to "put one foot in front of the other, ask for help when you need it."

So does it work? Does the message get through? "Oh yeah. I see it in their faces. They'll come right up to you and tell you how you made them feel. And to hear, 'You changed my life', from a teenager; that's something."

Laumann's first idol was gymnast Nadia Comaneci, the "perfect 10" in the 1976 Olympics. But Laumann's size—she stands 5 feet 10 inches—ruled out gymnastics. So she turned to track, but again, growth spurts put her out of the running. (Although she didn't have specific goals to compete in the Olympics in either gymnastics or track, she would have liked to have competed as far as she could if she had been suited for either sport.) At her sister's urging, she tried rowing and loved it. Daniele Laumann was on the National Rowing Team and within four months, so was Silken. Within two years, Silken had taken gold at the U.S. Championships and Pan American Games, and she and her sister won bronze rowing together in the 1984 Olympics in Los Angeles.

Silken Laumann holds up a paper hand during a children's charity fundraising event in a downtown Toronto McDonald's on May 16, 2000.

Her sister, now a lawyer in Halifax, didn't have the same drive to win, and Silken couldn't seem to find the right fit with another partner. At the 1988 Summer Games in Seoul, South Korea, Silken came seventh, and was so disappointed she thought about quitting. But her drive to win was still strong and she deeply believed if she worked hard enough, she could do it. So she struck out on her own, turning to the men's team, and its new coach, Mike Spracklen.

The first time Spracklen saw Silken work out, he predicted she'd medal in the Worlds. She did, coming second five months later. The next year, she came first, making her the best women's rower in the world and placing herself as a favourite for Olympic gold in Barcelona, Spain, the next year.

But the script changed when the German boat collided with Laumann. "That's the thing with life," says Laumann. "You can't control what's going to happen. But there are things you do have control over, and that's what you must focus on . . . You can't control what's going to happen in a competition. But you can control a race and be prepared for it, and that's what I always focus on as an athlete . . . I measure suc-cess not by winning; I measure success by doing my own personal best."

And that's why she was so happy with that bronze in Barcelona: "It was an amazing race. I did everything I could for that day; I controlled all that I could control for that day." Somebody did better than she and got gold, and she accepts that. While those medals are important to her, they're not what it's all about. Rather, she says, it's the process she went through to get them. The medals validate all her hard work and commitment, but beyond that, she says, they sit in a dresser drawer tarnishing. "I don't really treasure them. I treasure the memories, the friendships, the experiences," she says.

Despite the years of training, the early morning starts, and the late night fatigue, the closest Laumann got to Olympic gold was the trademark radiant smile she flashed when she won silver in her last competitive race in the 1996 Olympics in Atlanta, Georgia. Everybody likes a happy ending, and to those who don't know the depth of her character, it seems it just wasn't there for Laumann. "It was not the fairytale ending; it was real life ending," she says, reflecting on the close of her rowing career.

Laumann faced trials put before no other rower, and she had the spirit to leap over them. That painful injury changed her life. She has had seven operations and will likely face more. It also made her life more complicated. But it also added to her strength of character: "I'm happy with the person I am," she says.

Silken Laumann never did win that elusive gold medal, but she did win gold in the hearts of many Canadians for her courage that moment on the calm waters of a river in Spain. She didn't win, but she wasn't defeated.

This athlete supports:

Olympic Aid

375 Magna Drive

Aurora, ON L4G 7L6

e-mail: orna@olympicaid.org

Ronald McDonald Children's Charities of Canada

McDonald's Place

Toronto, ON M3C 3L4

e-mail: rmcc@mcdonalds.ca

Diane Jones Konihowski
Coming Full Circle

BORN: MARCH 7, 1951
VANCOUVER, BRITISH COLUMBIA

Every Friday morning, the pretty little blonde girl would gather the neighbourhood children together for a show. Their moms would sit in the backyard sipping coffee, cheering them on as they danced and sang their hearts out. Of course, Diane was the star of the show with her gymnastics performances.

And that was the three-time Olympian's first taste of sport. At age five, she joined a gymnastics club in Saskatoon. But by the time she reached her teens, it was clear the slender athlete was just too tall to compete. So she turned to basketball, volleyball, and, the sport that would make her famous, track and field.

"All I ever wanted to do was track and field," says Jones Konihowski, at 51 still one of Canada's most-recognized female sports figures. It all started at a church picnic. That's where former Olympic athlete Bob Adam first saw Diane run—and win every race. He knew she had something special and offered to be her coach.

"I wasn't a very good spectator," Jones Konihowski told writer Pat Rediger when interviewed for his book *Great Canadian Athletes*. "I couldn't watch, I had to be doing things. It wasn't

unusual for me to go to a track meet and enter 11 events." That drive for variety made the five-event pentathlon the ideal challenge for her.

By the time her professional days were over, she had competed in three Olympics, won gold at the 1975 and 1979 Pan American Games as well as the 1978 Commonwealth Games, set world records in the pentathlon twice, and was named to the Canadian Olympic Hall of Fame. She was also made a member of the Order of Canada for her contributions to athletics. Over the course of an athletic career that has spanned nearly three decades, she created a legacy that remains strong and valid today. Female athletes still come up to her on the street in awe. "It amazes me that people just come up and recognize me and know my name."

And why not? Her accomplishments and commanding presence in the media spotlight help draw a generation of young women struggling with their role in society into sport. Jones Konihowski was a well-known name in a popular sport when she first made it to the national stage in 1969. She used her prominence to promote the sport and teach women and young girls that they, too, could make it. Jones Konihowski says she wanted them to discover the joys and the lessons all sport has to offer. She wanted to inspire them to pursue their own goals—both in sports and in life. "At the time you're living it, you don't really realize the impact you have, it's not until you get older that you see what you've done for your sport."

Track and field is a particularly tough sport, whether you're a man or a woman. It's not a team sport, so, as Jones Konihowski says, you must rely on yourself even more, because there are no team members to motivate you. And self-motivated she was. "I had a goal, I wanted to be the best in the world. My goal was to be the number one pentathelete in the world." It took nine years to get there, but at 27 years of age, she did. "It was a fabulous accomplishment."

But there were times she'd set a goal, and fall short. Jones Konihowski was devastated to place 10th at the 1970 Commonwealth games. She began to have doubts about her abilities. Then she

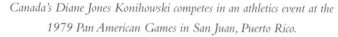

Canada's Diane Jones Konihowski competes in an athletics event at the 1979 Pan American Games in San Juan, Puerto Rico.

didn't make the 1971 Pan American Games team. Frustrated, she stopped training hard, gained weight, and became depressed.

It was a rough time, but the turning point came went she met an assistant coach named Bob Meldrum at a pre-Olympic meet. He gave her a pep talk, and told her that success is as much about your state of mind and your belief in yourself as it is about physical ability. The message came at a time when she needed it most. She dropped weight, trained hard, and ran fast enough to be named to the Olympic team. "All the way through, I've been really lucky having people interested in me, willing to work with me, and I think that's important," she told Rediger. And it taught her the importance of perseverance. "You can do anything you want if you have the passion and desire. And you have to be willing to discipline yourself."

When you're an athlete, being named to the Olympic team is the best feeling in the world—a sensation she was privileged to have experienced three times. The first was in Munich in 1972. "It was very exciting. My first opportunity to compete against the big, hairy, muscular Germans and Austrians. It was scary."

She placed 10th that year, setting a personal best and also showing that she wasn't afraid to compete against the world's best. She also knew she had to improve if she wanted to beat them, but also believed if she worked harder, she could do it. For her, it was all about the sport—the thrill of competition. "It was a simpler time; the games weren't so motivated by money and commercialism. It was so nice," she drawls. "I don't like what the Olympics have become, they've just become a big business."

Four years later there was Montreal. Jones Konihowski was a medal favourite, but placed sixth. "I was very mad at myself. I really blew it." She says she spent too much time promoting the sport and not enough time training. "I was mentally and physically soft and unfocused."

At the 1978 Commonwealth Games in Edmonton, she set a new games record in the pentathlon. Queen Elizabeth II presented her with her gold medal in front of her family and before a hometown crowd. Now ranked number one in the world, she was named Canada's Female Athlete of the Year for a second time.

But she still had goals in life. She set her sites on the Moscow Olympics. She moved to New Zealand with her husband, former Edmonton Eskimos wide receiver John Konihowski, where there would be no distractions from her training. She was in top form, and everyone predicted she'd be standing on the Olympic medal podium. But it was not meant to be. On April 23 she got a call from a Canadian reporter asking for her reaction to the fact Canada was joining the United States in a boycott of the games. She was shattered—her dream of Olympic Gold gone.

Today, she says her biggest regret in life is that she turned down a personal invitation to attend the games anyway. But, faced with death threats and harassment of her family and friends, she felt it just wouldn't be safe to go. After that, the Olympic bug left her. "It was taken away from me and I wasn't able to prove how good I was."

It took 18 months to regain her passion for the sport. By then, she had a young family and her priorities had changed. It was now more important to

instill a love of sport in others than to pursue her own medal dreams. She turned to coaching and teaching with the Canadian Track and Field Association and the National Training Centre, working with athletes in all sports. Until 2001, she worked at the National Sports Centre in Calgary, where she promoted sports and headed up fundraising and public relations efforts. But Jones Konihowski was to get one final shot at the Olympics.

Twenty-eight years after she first entered the Olympic stadium as an athlete, she returned as Chef-de-Mission to the 2000 Sydney Olympics. That meant she was responsible for ensuring all aspects of the team's needs—from medical requirements to media interviews—

Diane Jones Konihowski with youths at the Alberta Adolescent Recovery Centre.

69

were met. "I just had a ball. For me, it was a wonderful way for me to close the circle. I'm very content."

Today, Jones Konihowski has a new career. She's a businesswoman and, like everything she's tackled over the years, she is throwing herself into her latest venture. Premier Executive Suites, the company she founded with her husband, furnishes and leases condominiums for the long-term use of corporate executives. With offices in Halifax, Montreal, and Calgary, and with Jones Konihowski at the helm as president, the company is thriving. "I jumped in with both feet and I'm doing all aspects of the business. It's a huge learning curve," she says. Between meetings and refurbishing condos, Jones Konihowski makes time to exercise. "I'll never let myself slide for too long."

This athlete supports:
Alberta Adolescent
Recovery Centre
3o3 Forge Road SE
Calgary, AB T2H 0S9

Cam Neely
Cancer Crusader

Born: June 6, 1965
Comox, British Columbia

He was a brutish force who played hard and tough, but only on the ice. Caring, giving, kind, and selfless, this too is Cam Neely. The NHL hockey star who pummelled opponents for 10 years with the Boston Bruins is now a businessman and a philanthropist dedicated to making life a little better for cancer patients and their families.

"I'm a Gemini—a split personality —that explains it," says Neely with a laugh. "There's no doubt I grew up with a bad temper, and it certainly helped the way I played hockey. Off the ice, people assumed I'm this mean guy. But I think that's worn off now."

Most certainly. After all, the only checks Neely cares about these days are those made out to the Cam Neely Foundation, which has scored $10 million since it was created in 1995 and has built a cozy haven for cancer patients and their families at the New England Medical Center.

Now turning to other building projects and cancer research, Neely is tireless and committed when it comes to the struggle against cancer. It comes from the heart. It comes out of love. For this hockey hero, life after sports is about paying tribute to parents who taught him all about kindness and giving.

Michael Neely passed away December 12, 1993. Marlene Neely died on November 21, 1987. Both lost battles to cancer.

They are the inspiration for the Neely House, a welcoming and comfortable home providing shelter and support for families whose loved ones are undergoing cancer treatment. The exquisite, 14,500 square-foot bed-and-breakfast-style house is actually located within the walls of the New England Medical Center, an elevator ride away from the treatment and patient rooms.

Born out of deep understanding of the toll cancer takes, not just on the patient but on the whole family, the $2-million Neely House takes up one floor of the hospital, with 16 self-contained apartments, two large living rooms, two dining rooms, two kitchens, and laundry facilities, and provides the opportunity for families to talk to others facing similar situations. More than 650 families have taken advantage of the home since it opened, staying anywhere from one night to nearly a year. They pay merely $10 a night, and only if they can afford it.

"My main concern was I didn't want patients and families to feel like they were staying in the hospital," says

Neely. "We made darn sure that when you walk off the elevator on that floor, you feel like you're in a high-end hotel." House manager Patricia Rowe says people are overwhelmed by what the house offers. Letters, cards, and donations pour in from appreciative former guests, who often come back to visit and reunite with those they met during their stay.

"The home is often mistakenly called the Cam Neely House," says Neely. "But it isn't. It's the Neely House. It's in memory of our parents." The project has been a family affair. The Cam Neely

Foundation, which Neely formed with the home in mind, is headed by Neely's brother, Scott, as executive director. Two sisters, Christine and Shaun, who live in the family's hometown of Maple Ridge, B.C., provided support, ideas, and suggestions.

"I'm sure my mother and father are very proud of what we've been able to accomplish with a lot of other people. I'm sure they would be very proud of the job they have done in raising good kids. Kids that care," says Neely.

Marlene and Michael Neely were,

Cam Neely, 1991.

quite simply, parents who cared, making sure their four children got to their various activities, even if it meant getting up at the crack of dawn and spending hours in cold arenas. It paid off.

Neely began his NHL career in his home province with the Vancouver Canucks when they made him their first-round draft pick in 1983. He would play for the Canucks for three years before being traded to the Bruins in 1986 in exchange for points-machine Barry Pedersen and future first-round-pick Glen Weasley. At the time, many believed the Bruins got robbed, but it soon became obvious the trade was a steal for Boston. With the Bruins, Neely became a hard-nosed right winger known to slam opponents into the boards with his devastating checks and bring fans to their feet with his spectacular goals. He was considered the best power forward in the NHL for a decade.

It was Neely's style of play, in fact, that gave birth to the term "power forward." The six-foot one-inch, 220-pound player was such a force on the ice that Boston Bruins general manager Harry Sinden decided to come up with a new name for Neely's position.

The *Boston Globe* described Neely as "all about power—power to score, power to punch, power to punish,"—a player who "used the power of his personality to turn on Boston hockey fans like no player since Bobby Orr."

In his first season with the Bruins, the mighty Neely burst forward with 36 goals, a team high, and followed it up the next season with 40 goals. He would go on to record two 50-plus goal seasons in 1989-90 and 1990-91.

Between games, Neely was one of the most visible professional athletes in the Boston area, making appearances for numerous charities, lending support where needed. He would later be listed by the *Boston Globe* as one of New

The Neely House opening ceremony ribbon cutting (left to right): Dr. Thomas O'Donnell, Jr. (NEMC president/CEO), Christine Neely Lisowsky, Shaun Neely Craig, Cam Neely, Scott Neely, and Dr. David Schenkein (director, Cancer Center NEMC).

England's top sports figures of the century. This laudable sideline would soon take on a much bigger role in his life.

In a play-off game in 1991 against Pittsburgh, the hard-hitting Neely took a crushing hit himself. It would be the start of a series of physical woes leading eventually to a premature end to a dazzling hockey career. He received a knee to the thigh, resulting in the development of a rare condition called myositis ossificans, which caused part of the thigh muscle to calcify.

For the next two seasons, Neely was limited to 22 games, but he still managed to slip in 20 goals and 10 assists, and added four playoff goals in the 1993 playoffs. The number of per-game goals was incredible, particularly since Neely had played in great pain for many of those matches.

He made an amazing comeback in 1993–4, hitting the 50-goal mark for the third time, and in only 44 games. Only Wayne Gretzky has done it faster. Neely's grit and determination to repeatedly get back in the game after devastating injuries earned him the Masterton Trophy in 1993–4, but a blow to the knee that year sent him to the sidelines for the playoffs. Intensive rehabilitation got him back on the ice

for a shortened 1994–5 season, during which he scored 27 goals in 42 games, but the next year was Neely's last. A degenerative hip condition surfaced that would prove to be the last straw. On September 5, 1996, at age 31, the fan favourite retired.

In all, the five-time all-star scored 395 goals and 299 assists in only 726 games. But his retirement would be the start of even greater accomplishments. He started a family, founded the Neely House, and would become a vice-president at GenuOne, a start-up company offering unique technologies to help businesses protect themselves against counterfeiting, grey-market diversion, royalty fraud, and intellectual property theft. The hockey pro turned savvy, self-taught businessman has become a powerhouse in a new arena.

"Starting a family after my hockey career was probably the best thing for me, mentally. It's very difficult to leave something, anything, especially a sport, when it's not on your terms. Anyone who is a parent knows it's the best thing in the world."

The next best thing for Neely, it seems, is giving. "As a professional athlete, you get asked to do many charity-related functions or go see sick children in hospital. And just because of what you do, you're able to walk in there and maybe put a smile on someone's face and perhaps give them a memory they can cherish. It's a pretty special ability to have. How could you not want to help people?"

Although he now rarely plays hockey —"I only have so many miles left on my hip and I'd rather use them playing with my kids"—Neely won't retire from putting smiles on faces.

This athlete supports:

Cam Neely Foundation

30 Winter Street, Second Floor

Boston, MA 02108

The Olympians

Curtis Joseph
"He's the Man"

BORN: APRIL 29, 1967
KESWICK, ONTARIO

You can read all the impressive statistics you want about hockey great Curtis Joseph, but they will tell you little about the former Maple Leafs goaltender. Talk to 14-year-old Josh Tervit and in three words, he can tell you everything. "Let me put this in teenage words," says Josh. "He's the man." Josh is not referring to Joseph's hockey skills. He's not talking at all about Joseph's style or stardom on ice. He's talking about "the man" off the ice, the one with a big heart who gives kids like Josh an opportunity they savour for years, maybe even a lifetime.

Josh is one of "Cujo's Kids." He's among more than 500 children who each year become guests of Joseph in a private box at the Air Canada Centre in Toronto. For every Maple Leafs game during the year, including exhibition action, the regular season, and the playoffs, Joseph invites 16 seriously ill children and their families to rink-side for the thrill of an NHL game. It's a thrill with a therapeutic touch for these children, sending sinking spirits soaring, stirring self-esteem, and making a suffering child feel special.

When Josh received the invitation, "he was beside himself," recalls mom Kate Tervit, who will never forget August 13, 2001, the day Josh was hit by a car while riding his bike with two friends. Among his injuries were two broken legs, a collapsed lung, and most devastating, a severe head injury.

"He couldn't believe something good was happening after all the bad that had happened," says Kate. "It gave him hope for better days. It gave us the chance to enjoy something as a family ... It boosted Josh's confidence at being able to provide this opportunity for us and see that he could negotiate through the crowds and deal with the noise and excitement. I don't remember smiling so much in a long time."

Joseph has been eliciting those smiles for years. He and his wife, Nancy, started the program in Edmonton in 1995 with the "Cujo's Cloud Nine" sky-box when Joseph played for the Edmonton Oilers. In 1998, when he was signed by the Toronto Maple Leafs, Joseph brought the program with him, where it became "Cujo's Kids." The children are selected by the Hospital of Sick Children in Toronto, the London Health Sciences Centre, and McMaster University Medical Centre in Hamilton.

"For many kids, it's an escape to jump into another world outside the hospital and their frequent treatments," explains Bev McDonald, child life professional practice leader at the London Health Sciences Centre. "It gives them a surge of energy. The kids chosen here will do what it takes to get on that bus. It gives them a fresh outlook. They get to experience something they have never experienced or may never experience again. Most important, it helps them forget they are sick, if only for a short time." And that makes Cujo's Kids the winners of every Leafs game played at home.

For children with cancer, Joseph brings hockey to the hospital. At the Hospital for Sick Children, youngsters can receive treatment in a specially equipped room designed and decorated to replicate the Leafs' dressing room. It's called Cujo's Crease, and it helps take the ouch out of painful procedures. For ill children, this is what Joseph is all about. Most don't even know that Joseph is one of the best all-around goaltenders in the NHL and was the backbone of the

Toronto Maple Leafs goaltender Curtis Joseph makes the save on New Jersey Devils winger Turner Stevenson during game three of the NHL Eastern Conference semi-finals in Toronto, on May 1, 2001.

Maple Leafs. It matters little to them that he set a franchise record for wins in 1999–2000 and won the King Clancy Memorial Trophy the same year.

They likely couldn't tell you that, in Edmonton, Joseph was named the Oilers' most valuable player as well as the most popular player in 1996–7, that he was just as popular the next season, or that he has been a finalist for the Vezina Trophy for outstanding goalic three times. What Cujo's Kids appreciate perhaps more than most is Joseph's gutsy approach to the game, his competitiveness, and his perseverance. Joseph never believes he's beaten, Mark Messier once said on ESPN's Sportzone, describing the elite netminder.

Born in Keswick, Ontario, on April 29, 1967, Joseph fulfilled a boyhood dream by playing with the Maple Leafs. His hometown is about an hour's drive north of Toronto, and many Leaf players were his heroes growing up. Playing for the team was an honour. The 35-year-old goalie's NHL hockey career was launched while playing for the University of Wisconsin, where he attracted attention by earning both rookie and player of the year awards. He spent his first six NHL seasons with the St. Louis Blues.

In 1995, the 5-foot 10-inch, 188-pound Joseph arrived in Edmonton, where he rejuvenated the Oilers, gave them a chance at a playoff spot, and became a huge fan favourite. His skill earned him the position of starting goaltender for Team Canada in the 1996 World Championships and the 1996 World Cup, both culminating in silver medals.

Joseph's 1996–7 season in Edmonton was one for the record books. He accumulated the most shutouts for both himself and his team in one season with six, including stopping 52 shots to tie the Stanley Cup Champions, the Detroit Red Wings, at a score of 0–0 on December 10, 1996. The double shutout game was the first ever in team history.

The Oilers went on to a 1–0 win on January 31, 1997, when the team hosted the New York Islanders as part of the regular season. Joseph was given a standing ovation. By the time Joseph came to Toronto in 1998, his unorthodox style was well known. Using a combination of standup and butterfly, Joseph has lightning-quick reflexes that, in 1994–5, ranked fifth best among goaltenders, according to the *Sporting News Hockey Yearbook*.

Toronto Maple Leafs Curtis Joseph takes Ryan Kavanagh, 12, for a spin during a charity skate fundraising event at the Air Canada Centre in Toronto on November 28, 1999.

His unusual movements on ice and fierce protection of the net gave birth to his nickname "Cujo," after the mad beast in the Stephen King novel of the same name. His teammates felt he suited the moniker, which, coincidentally, is also the first two letters in his first and last names. Despite the nickname, Joseph has been called "one of hockey's nicest people" by *Sports Forecaster,* as well as a "weird goalie" who handles the puck like it's a live grenade.

In 1998, this weird goalie was named

to the Canadian Olympic team, the first Olympics with full NHL participation. Unfortunately, Joseph didn't get to play, and Canada was beaten by the Czech Republic in a shoot-out in the semifinals before losing the bronze-medal game to Finland. But in 2002, Joseph once again made the roster of hockey superstars to go to the Olympic Winter Games. This time, the Olympic experience would be bittersweet. Joseph was chosen as starting goaltender, but after a 5–2 loss to Sweden in the first game, he was pulled and never given another chance. With Martin Brodeur in net, the team went on to win the nation's first hockey gold in 50 years in a phenomenal series that became a highlight of the games. Shortly after Salt Lake City, Joseph broke a bone in his hand and he was again sidelined.

But what makes this hockey hero great is less about stopping pucks than it is about the way he stops to reflect on his good fortune in life, on the ice and off. He's grateful for his hockey career, but, more important, he's grateful for

83

his wife and four children. He's a young father who knows what it means to have healthy children. He feels lucky and so he gives sick children a chance to feel lucky too. Cujo's Kids are treated like royalty in the private box with finger food, soda pop, autographed souvenirs to take home, and often a visit by Nancy and her children, or even Joseph himself.

For Josh, the trip was especially memorable because he was allowed to bring the two friends who were with him when he was injured. Although they weren't hurt physically, Josh wanted to do something to help them heal after witnessing the horrible accident. "How do you say thanks for bringing such joy?" asks Kate, who was undergoing treatment for breast cancer when Josh was injured, compounding the family tragedy. "I'm so impressed that Curtis Joseph takes the time to have his life and his success touch others." But then, that's precisely what makes Curtis Joseph "the man."

In early July, Joseph broke the hearts of many Toronto Maple Leaf hockey fans when he left the Leafs and signed with the Detroit Red Wings.

This athlete supports:
Children's Wish Foundation
of Canada
National Office
95 Bayly Street, Suite 404
Ajax, ON L1S 7K8
website: www.childrenswish.ca

Catriona Le May Doan
God, Family, and Then Sport

BORN: DECEMBER 23, 1970
SASKATOON, SASKATCHEWAN

It was supposed to be her turn for a medal. It wouldn't be gold, but going into her final race at the 1994 Winter Olympics in Norway, Saskatoon-born speed skater Catriona Le May Doan was confident a bronze medal in the 500-metre sprint was within her grasp. She was 23, it was her second Olympics, and she had six years of world competition under her skate laces. With a nearly perfect race, she'd be on the podium.

She got a good start at the gun, but halfway through the 40-second dash, her skate caught an edge and she tumbled to the ice like a rag doll. Her Olympic dream was dead. Or so she thought. "It was a horrible moment at the time, but in retrospect, something very positive came out of it. I found my faith," she says. "That has made me a better person, which in turn has made me a better speed skater."

A devout Christian, the Olympic gold medallist and two-time Canadian female athlete of the year uses her status as a top-flight athlete to share her faith, challenging and motivating people to achieve their full potential. In an opinion piece written last year, Southam News columnist Lawrence Martin called Le May Doan the best role model

that female athletics had produced since figure skater Barbara Ann Scott or skier Nancy Greene. "She's the best in the world in her sport; she's as pure as the driven snow; she's drop-dead gorgeous —and, unlike so many stars we know, she isn't even a head case."

This kind of assessment makes the bilingual, four-time Olympian shift awkwardly and stare down at her special clapskates. Even after 20 years in the spotlight, she's uncomfortable with the suggestion she's anything more than an average Canadian woman, working hard and doing her best.

As a kid growing up in Saskatoon, she attended church intermittently and had no strong religious convictions. Her passion was sports. She joined the local speed-skating club at age 10 and raced with her sister on an outdoor track even when the temperature was minus 40 °C. Her sister quit the club after several years, but Le May Doan carried on and made the national team straight out of high school. She ran track in high school and competed as a national-level hurdler and heptathlete from 1993 to 1995, when she gave it up to focus exclusively on speed skating.

Then came the devastating fall at Lillehammer, Norway, and a depression

Catriona Le May Doan of Saskatoon, Saskatchewan, powers around a turn in the women's 1,000-metre speed skating final at the Salt Lake City Olympic Games on February 17, 2002.

she couldn't shake—until one day when, while driving around Calgary, she saw a billboard for Athletes in Action, an international sports ministry that helps athletes get to know God. On an impulse, she met with staff members and within a few weeks became a believer. "It changed how I looked at sport and at life. I can look at a gold medallist and at someone who's fallen and see no difference at all. A person shouldn't change just because they've been on the medal podium."

Since then she has had her time on the podium. As her faith blossomed, so did her skating. She became the Canadian sprint champion in 1996 and won both gold and silver medals in the 500 metres at that year's world championships. She followed up with a silver at the world championships in 1997 and earned the title "Fastest Woman on Ice" in Nagano, Japan, when she blazed to gold in the 500 metres, smashing the Olympic record in the process. Then she

tacked on a bronze medal in the 1,000 metres. Her joyous reaction, her graceful elegance, and her victory lap carrying the Canadian flag captured the hearts of Canadians and clinched her selection as the 1998 Canadian Female Athlete of the Year.

She took the honour again in 2001 by breaking her own world record and winning almost every race she entered. She captured four World Cup gold medals and was unbeaten in 17 of the 18 races at 500 metres she entered leading

87

up to the Salt Lake City Olympics. Le May Doan was tagged as one of the nation's sure bets during the games, and she did not disappoint. She used her unique combination of grace, elegance, and brute strength to win gold and become the first Canadian to successfully defend an individual gold medal in an Olympic sport.

But she also shone as flag bearer for the opening ceremonies and proved herself an excellent ambassador during hundreds of media interviews that followed. When it comes time for balloting for the 2002 Female Athlete of the Year, the image of Le May Doan gliding on the ice after her win, clad in her mottled red and black race suit—wearing her husband's black cowboy hat and waving the Canadian flag—will be difficult to forget.

People constantly ask her how she can be so competitive, so aggressive, while remaining a Christian. She flashes a megawatt smile and says simply that she has a gift, and she has to use it to the best of her abilities.

Le May Doan's victories are not something she flaunts. Visitors to the Calgary home she shares with her rodeo steer-wrestling husband, Bart Doan, won't find anything on the walls or the coffee tables that even hint she has been dubbed the fastest woman on ice.

There are lots of candles, family photos, and a beautiful bronze sculpture that Bart's grandfather won at the Calgary Stampede in 1944, but nothing to do with skating. Surprisingly, given her religious convictions, there are no crosses. "Our faith is something that we are trying to show in how we live and treat others," she says.

The skater's Olympic medals are handy in case she needs to show them at a school or take them to a corporate function, but everything else, from her retired skates to her certificates of participation in countless events, are on display down the road at the Calgary Olympic Park. "Speed skating is so much a part of me, I don't need the reminders around. It's what I do. It's what I love."

But whether she's speaking to schoolchildren or making an appearance with Athletes in Action sharing her beliefs, Le May Doan makes it clear the sport is not who she is. If it were all gone tomorrow, she says, she'd still be comfortable with herself and enjoy the love of her husband and her family. It's all about perspective. "I'm a speed skater, but take away the speed skater,

I'm still Catriona. The biggest thing in my life is my faith and then my husband and my family."

Her integrity, dedication, and commitment to excellence put her in demand as a speaker. She laughs easily and especially enjoys talking to young children. "Kids look at you in awe. They want to hear your stories and see the medals. You make it real to them. It's not just something they see on television. I challenge them. If I can make it, why can't they?"

During these presentations, she always makes it clear that on the path to becoming a world champion she sold vacuum cleaners, worked as a secretary for her father, and spent several years as a waitress at Red Lobster. "I don't put myself in another category. I don't see myself as a superstar. I know people watch me, but I still go down to the grocery store in sweats with my hair a mess," she says. The only member of her family not to have multiple university degrees, Le May Doan says she regrets not making time for college but believes the education she has received travelling around the globe has helped compensate.

When she began winning medals, she was approached by numerous organizations interested in using her profile to promote their causes. She has spoken on behalf of several athletics groups but is especially proud of her association with the Spina Bifida and Hydrocephalus Association of Canada. Spina bifida is the most common birth

Catriona Le May Doan leads the Canadian team into the stadium during the opening ceremonies for the XIX Olympic Winter Games in Salt Lake City, Utah, February 8, 2002.

defect in Canada. She first learned about it in high school when the son of a track coach was diagnosed with it. She saw firsthand the struggles it created for a family and pledged to do whatever she could to make more people aware of the disorder. She has made a public service announcement on behalf of the organization and speaks to various groups about the importance of folic acids during the first months of pregnancy.

With both her gold medal from Salt Lake City and the 2002 World Cup title in hand, Le May Doan says she plans to compete for one more year and then work on beginning a family. Even then, she doesn't want to be too far away from the ice. After indulging her love of golf and her passion for horses, she might like to try her hand at sports commentating or at least continue to speak to business and other groups about goal-setting and her faith.

This athlete supports:

Athletes in Action
National Headquarters
PO Box 300
Vancouver, BC V6C 2X3
e-mail: aia@athletesinaction.com

Spina Bifida and
Hydrocephalus Association
of Canada
167 Lombard Avenue, Suite 167
Winnipeg, MB R3B 0T6

Simon Whitfield
The People's Champion

BORN: MAY 16, 1975
KINGSTON, ONTARIO

It has been called the greatest moment in Canadian sport since Paul Henderson slipped the puck past Vladislav Tretiak to give Canada the victory in the 1972 Summit series against the Russians. Picture this: A skinny, virtually unknown kid from Kingston finishes the swim and bicycle legs of the men's triathlon in 26th place, but then blows past the competition in the 10-kilometre run to win Olympic gold on the home stretch.

Simon Whitfield's dramatic come-from-behind victory at the 2000 Summer Olympics in Sydney, Australia, captured the imagination of the nation and catapulted the easy-going 24-year-old from obscurity into the forefront of sports in Canada. At the time, Whitfield was ranked just 13th in the world and was as unfamiliar to Canadians as the sport in which he was competing.

The triathlon, consisting of a 1,500-metre swim, a 40-kilometre bike race, and a 10-kilometre run, was hugely popular in Australia, France, and other parts of the world, but it never really piqued the interest of average Canadians. Until Sydney. Until Canadians saw Whitfield pull away from the middle of the pack and pass the leaders, one by one. By the time he delivered his fantas-tic finish to push past leader Stephan Vukovic of Germany with just 350 metres to go, Canadians were hooked. And if the spectacular victory combining strength, endurance, conditioning, and determination weren't enough to win over every Canuck heart, Whitfield brought the hold-outs on board by sobbing uncontrollably as the national anthem was played and the flag was raised during the medal ceremony.

Since Sydney, the country has discovered triathlon, and sport in general could not have found a better ambassador. Whitfield is an articulate, fun-loving patriot who is prepared to do the unexpected. At the 2001 World Cup Triathlon in Toronto, he wrapped himself in a Canadian flag as he danced across the finish line. He then shook off race officials who tried to drag him to media interviews, choosing instead to sign autographs and chat earnestly with the fans who'd come to cheer him on.

It's not much different at any Whitfield event. He is the people's champion. The gangly, free-spirited 27-year-old wants to talk to people about the sport he loves. As a result, participation in the swim-bike-run sport has grown faster than a Donovan Bailey 100-metre dash.

Before his Olympic victory, an estimated 50,000 Canadians were participating in some form of triathlon. Since then, every province is reporting increases in participation, some as much as 50 percent. Whitfield has helped fan the flames of success by actively supporting Triathlon Canada's Kids of Steel, a program designed to offer kids and young adults the opportunity to experience the sport of triathlon in a positive environment. The distances in this program are much shorter than those in adult triathlons and change as participants mature. Most kids are fit enough to finish a Kids of Steel triathlon successfully and have fun at the same time. "It's a great opportunity for kids to participate in sport, and that's all that matters," he says. "From there, whether they stay in triathlon or branch out, they have a foundation of fun."

Whitfield's first triathlon was a Kids of Steel event at Sharbot Lake, Ontario,

Canadian triathlon winner Simon Whitfield celebrates as he crosses the finish line in 1:48:24 to win the gold medal during the Sydney Summer Olympics, September 17, 2000.

in 1987. He was just 12 years old, but his penchant for off-beat humour was already evident. He recalls cracking up competitors by racing in boxer shorts that had little cows on them. Whitfield liked everything about that first experience and quickly became a triathlon junkie. He won his first Kids of Steel race in 1991 and four years later took the Canadian Junior National Triathlon Championship.

Whitfield raced in events around the globe in the run-up to Sydney, finishing ninth in the World Championships in Perth, Australia, in 1997, and seventh in the Worlds when they were held in Montreal in 1999. He blew a tire and couldn't finish at the Worlds in May 2000 but placed second at World Cup events that year in Rio de Janeiro and Corner Brook, Newfoundland. As though to prove his Olympic victory was not a fluke, during 2001 he won races in Victoria, Toronto, and the United States. He was also the toast of Edmonton during the world championships, despite his sixth-place finish.

"Sometimes I think of Simon as a hyperactive kid almost—but with a huge heart," Lance Watson, Whitfield's Victoria-based coach, told the *Toronto Star*. "He's always going on, always jok-ing, having a good time. But when it comes time to focus, he's all there."

"He couldn't be a better Olympic champion," added rival and long-time friend Chris McCormack. "He's not fake. If he placed last, he'd be the same." Whitfield takes his it's-not-whether-you're-first-or-last message into schools across the country and the kids eat it up. "You have a responsibility to yourself to be healthy and to be fit and to love sport," he told awestruck students at a B.C. elementary school a few months before the 2001 World Championships in Edmonton. "I think if you can all take from the Olympic Games that message, that's what's most important. It's not about winning gold medals—it's about being healthy and meeting people and great experiences."

To drive the point home, Whitfield always carries the participant's medal given to athletes who compete at the Olympics. He says it sits right beside the gold medal on the mantel in his Victoria home, because "it was just as important to be there" as to win.

Asked about whether or not a triathlete in training should specialize in one aspect of the sport, Whitfield tells students that although coaches encouraged him to stick to running, his dad

94

wouldn't let him get serious about any one sport. "My dad just thought it would be a lot better for me as a person to not specialize and just enjoy any sport and not worry about the competitive nature of it," he says. "That's what triathlon so embodies."

Whitfield hasn't let public appearances or corporate talks take precedence over his first love—training and competition—but he's been generous with his time for schools, perhaps because he doesn't want kids to make the same mistake he did. "I didn't do particularly well at school," he told CBC's *Inside Track* shortly after his Olympic win. "I regret not being focused on school and not having the determination to do well. I kind of relied on my sporting ability and that was a bit shortsighted." Despite spending two years at a discipline-oriented boarding school in Australia that was supposed to kickstart his academic motivation, Whitfield said he continued to struggle and still has gaps in his knowledge base that wouldn't exist if he had paid more attention in school.

If the time down under failed to spark his academic interest, it stoked his competitive fires to the point that the Aussies tried to lure him into competing for Australia. Thankfully, he resisted the temptation and returned to Canada.

Another cause he's proud to champion is the drive to find a cure for multiple sclerosis (MS), an often-disabling disease of the central nervous system. Its symptoms are highly variable and unpredictable, but can include vision and speech problems, extreme fatigue,

Canadian Olympic gold medallist Simon Whitfield and Rhiannon MacLean do their part at the Daily Bread food bank in preparation for the 2000 Thanksgiving weekend in Toronto, Ontario.

95

lack of balance and coordination, and even paralysis. Whitfield's uncle, Hugh Ames, has battled the disease for more than 20 years.

"He inspires me to do my best," Whitfield says on an MS promotional video, describing Ames as a confidant who knows most of his secrets and the names of all of the girls he ever went out with. "He runs an Olympic triathlon every day, overcoming the obstacles MS puts in his way. Any hardship or obstacle I face pales in comparison." In addition to the video and speaking on behalf of the MS Society, Whitfield has helped promote the MS bike rally in B.C., which in 2001 raised $225,000 at five different sites.

In the weeks after the terrorist attacks on the United States in 2001, Whitfield continued to show his compassionate side, appearing with other celebrities for a televised benefit by MuchMusic to raise money for the victims. In an interview afterwards, he said he hoped the atrocity would help teach people to be kind to one another. "Be a good person and lead a good life," he said. "If everyone tried to be a good person and did things honestly and responsibly, then none of this would happen."

Whitfield suffered two broken wrists and a broken collarbone in a bike crash in April 2002 but erased any fears it would have a long-term impact on his career by winning a World Cup event in Edmonton in mid-July. Triathletes compete well into their 30s, so he's confident he'll be in the hunt for Olympic gold when the 2004 Games open in Athens, Greece.

This athlete supports:
Multiple Sclerosis Society
of Canada
250 Bloor Street E, Suite 1000
Toronto, ON M4W 3P9
website: www.mssociety.ca

Hayley Wickenheiser
Centre of Attention

BORN: AUGUST 12, 1978
SHAUNAVON, SASKATCHEWAN

Hayley Wickenheiser blushes when a young fan stops her on a Calgary street corner and tells her she's her hero. Her cheeks redden even more when the excited 13-year-old asks her what it's like to be the best female hockey player in the world.

"I'm just a farm girl from Saskatchewan and I play hockey," Wickenheiser responds with the kind of modesty that has led fans to embrace the 5-foot 10-inch poster girl for women's hockey as a national icon. "I work hard. I believe if you really want to do something, if you're willing to put the time and effort into it, it'll happen. It has for me, and it can for you, too." The light changes and the beaming teen races off to tell her friends about meeting the Olympic gold medallist. Wickenheiser hopes she will also share the message that a little hard work can go a long way.

And there's no question that Wick—as she's known to friends and teammates—works hard. Not only is she the leader of Team Canada's women's hockey squad, but she's also an Olympic softball outfielder and coordinator of her own one-on-one hockey and confidence-building clinic for young women. As if that weren't enough, she's also a mother pursuing a medical degree.

Big, strong, and explosively fast, her determined play in the corners and at the goal crease guided Team Canada to four gold medals at the World Championships, three gold medals in Three Nations Cup play, a silver medal at the 1998 Nagano Winter Olympics, and unforgettable gold at the Salt Lake City Games in 2002.

Whether she's on the ice or in the field, the pride of Shaunavon, Saskatchewan, has fire in her belly. She's passionate, intense, and always looking for new ways to improve and get past the competition. Shannon Miller, former Canadian National team and Olympic coach, says Wickenheiser's skills make her special, but it's an inner hunger, a fierce desire to win, that has helped her boost the profile of women's hockey over the past decade.

At 24, she already enjoys more success than many athletes achieve in a lifetime. But ask the woman in the number 22 jersey which accomplishment she's most proud of and the answer is instantaneous: It's her son, Noah. "He's the best thing that ever happened to me," she says, handing the two year old yet another small hockey stick from the endless supply sent to her by fans. "He may be a hockey player himself one day."

Hayley Wickenheiser (left) celebrates her second-period goal with teammates Geraldine Heaney (91) and Colleen Sostorics. Canada won the gold medal on February 21, 2002, with a 3–2 victory over the United States in Salt Lake City during the Winter Olympics.

Wickenheiser may be rough on the ice and fearless on the softball field, but during those rare moments when she's not running to a game, a practice, a speaking engagement, or a class, she's kicked-back casual about her life and her accomplishments. She doesn't see herself as a superstar nor as especially gifted because she plays both hockey and softball at the highest level. Those were the sports everybody played growing up on the Prairies, she explains. If you wanted your time on the field or on the ice, you had to play well.

Wickenheiser got her first pair of skates when she was just slightly older than her son is now. And like Wayne Gretzky, with whom she is frequently compared, she got her start in hockey on a backyard rink. She joined a boys' league at age five because there were no girls' teams, and she quickly established herself as an important player. As her skills improved under the guidance of her father, Tom, she scored more goals and attracted a lot of attention—not all of it good. On too many occasions, she says, she was forced to endure catcalls from parents who were upset she was taking a position away from a boy. "I always loved to play, so I developed thick skin early on and pushed through it."

When her family moved to Calgary in 1990, she joined a newly formed girls' peewee league and quickly became the city's top scorer. Her coach was Shannon Miller. At just age 12, she was invited to play for Alberta at the Canada Winter Games. She more than held her own against rival 16- and 17-year-old

99

girls and scored the winning goal in the gold-medal game.

At age 15, she made the national team, where her older teammates nick-named her "highchair Hayley," but she helped them win the 1994 world championship. The next year, as winter gave way to spring, she took just enough time away from hockey to play in the 1995 women's world softball championships. "It was always my dream when I was a kid to get to there in softball, and I actually thought I would play softball before I would play hockey in the Olympics. It turned out the other way around."

Returning her focus to hockey, she gradually assumed a leadership role on the team. With each medal-winning performance, she says, women's hockey gradually gained the respect of the "old boy's club." The respect blossomed into all-out flag-waving when women's hockey became an official event at the 1998 Olympic Winter Games. The importance of the moment was captured by Wick in a column she wrote on behalf of the team for Sun Media just before leaving for Nagano, Japan: "As female hockey players, we are grateful for the opportunity to live out our Olympic dreams. We only hope these

Olympics will encourage other young girls to get involved. So that some day they, too, may feel the pride of wearing that Maple Leaf."

Canada lost to their American archrivals in the gold-medal round, but Wickenheiser played well. She had the jersey she wore framed; it is now prominently displayed in her spacious baby-proofed Calgary condominium alongside mementos from many of the places she's played during her career.

Proving she is able to shift gears quickly, immediately after Nagano Wickenheiser traded the steel blades for the aluminum bat of Olympic softball. Playing as a utility outfielder, Wickenheiser travelled to Australia to become the second Canadian woman to do the Winter-Summer Olympic Games double. (Winnipeg's Clara Hughes, a bronze-medal cyclist at the 1996 Summer Olympics, became the third when she took to the speed skating track in Salt Lake City.)

"In hockey, I'm seen as the team leader," says Wickenheiser. "In softball, I'm still learning. I still have to prove myself." Her hockey prowess did not go unrecognized, and in 1998 she became the first woman skater to attend an NHL training camp, where she worked out with the Philadelphia Flyer rookies. She enjoyed the experience and the focus it put on women's hockey, but she says not once did she think of it as a step towards the NHL.

Women's hockey has come a long way since she first took to the ice, but Wickenheiser is most pleased with the grassroots development she sees. "When I played, I changed in the boiler room or the back of the car. Now people are used to seeing girls walking around a rink with a hockey bag and a stick."

To help keep the momentum going, in 2000, she organized the Wickenheiser One-on-One tour with her Czech-born boyfriend Tomas Pacina, a hockey coach at the Olympic Oval in Calgary. The 12-city event gave 5,000 players, aged nine and up, a one-hour session on the ice with their idol and another hour of chat and advice. "When I was growing up, there were no female role models for me. I had Gretzky and Messier to look up to. Now you see girls out there, and they're aware of national team players, they know names and faces now. That's kind of exciting."

Canadian national women's hockey team member Hayley Wickenheiser signs six-year-old Sarah Halpenny's jersey after a news conference to announce the final Olympic team roster in Calgary, November 20, 2001.

A huge fan of the work done by the Kids Cancer Care Foundation of Alberta, she frequently makes appearances at summer camps and recreational opportunities provided for children with cancer. For the past five years, she's also helped promote Dreams Take Flight, a program that sends terminally ill kids to Disneyland, courtesy of Air Canada.

She also finds school visits exciting. She estimates she's been to 40 schools in the Calgary area in the last two years. What does she tell the students? Believe in yourself. Find a passion and work hard at it. Pursue your dreams. Do what you love, not what someone else says you should do. "They may be clichés, but they are also simple truths. The world is complicated enough without trying to wrap up passion and desire in some complicated philosophy," says Wickenheiser.

Armed with those simple truths, Team Canada went to Salt Lake City in February 2002 as underdogs and emerged as gold medallists. The team stunned the heavily favoured United States and started Canadians on a celebration party that didn't end until long after the Canadian men captured gold three days later.

Wickenheiser, the squad's career scoring leader with 160 points in 108 games, was named the tournament's most valuable player and mused openly about trying to earn a spot on a European men's team at some point in the future. For now though, her sharpest focus is on her medical degree. "Dr. Wickenheiser" has a nice ring to it, she says. "Medicine is the only thing I can see myself doing other than [being] a full-time athlete. I enjoy helping people and think a lot of the challenges are similar to athletics. The intangibles are very similar and I also love a challenge."

This athlete supports:

Kids Cancer Care
Foundation of Alberta
609-14 Street NW, Suite 205
Calgary, AB T2N 2A1

Olympic Aid
375 Magna Drive
Aurora, ON L4G 7L6
e-mail: orna@olympicaid.org

Marianne Limpert
Silver Medal Blessing

BORN: OCTOBER 10, 1972
MATAGAMI, QUEBEC

Swimmer Marianne Limpert has won 20 national titles and 81 international medals, including a silver at the 1996 Olympics in Atlanta, but the perky 29-year-old's most-cherished prize can't be worn around her neck. It's a large coffee-table book on sushi—her favourite food—and it was given to her by the parents of a fellow swimmer to thank her for an astonishing act of kindness during the run-up to the 2000 Olympics in Sydney.

The oldest and most successful member of the women's team, Limpert had just qualified for her fifth Olympic event at the Canadian Summer Nationals when she looked across the pool and saw teammate Nadine Rolland in tears. The 25-year-old Montrealer had been just 1/100th of a second behind Limpert and 15-year-old Jenna Gresdal in the 50-metre freestyle, but that fraction was enough to sink her Olympic dream.

Slipping out of the water, the muscular 5-foot 11-inch Limpert decided she would try to throw her teammate a lifeline. She told her coach, Randy Bennett, that she wanted to give up her spot in the freestyle. The move took officials by surprise, but after signing a few documents, Roland had her trip to the Olympics. "I was so happy for her," says Limpert, shrugging, off the sacrifice during a break from a training camp in sunny Hawaii. "I know when I told her, I was all red in the face and feeling at least as good as she was. It was incredible."

The book from Rolland's parents came some weeks later and enjoys a place of honour on a coffee table in the apartment she rents in downtown Montreal. Limpert's medals, including the Olympic silver for the 200-metre individual medley, are stuffed willy-nilly into drawers of a living-room entertainment unit. "It's not about the medals. They're nice, but they don't define my existence. They are just symbols of a journey—a journey that requires the marriage of physical strength with mental toughness. When I'm successful, it's because I've been able to stay calm and focus on the goal at hand. It's also when I'm having the most fun."

Swimming Canada's Female Swimmer of the Year for 1996, 1997, and 2000 got her feet wet in Fredericton, where she was raised, but as a child she was more interested in frozen ponds than in heated pools. Her dream was to skate in the Olympics. A growth spurt put an end to the short skirts, makeup, and music, so at her grandfather's urging, she

Marianne Limpert competing in the swimming event at the 1992 Olympic Games in Barcelona.

took up swimming in earnest. With hunky Olympic double-gold medallist Alex Baumann as a role model, Limpert made a name for herself on the swim circuit in Eastern Canada and joined the national team in 1990. She claimed her first national medals—two golds, a silver, and two bronzes—the following year.

Big things were expected of Limpert at her first Olympics in Barcelona, but she was hit by a case of nerves and knew from the second she hit the water she didn't have a chance. She finished sixth. She thought briefly about quitting, but decided instead to use the experience as motivation. And it worked. Her performances improved and her confidence grew. She went to the podium for a silver medal and three bronze medals at the 1994 Commonwealth Games in Victoria and claimed five silver medals and one bronze at the 1995 Pan American Games held in Mar del Plata, Argentina.

But as the Atlanta Games loomed, the buzz was not about steady Marianne Limpert, the veteran swimmer, but about Joanne Malar, a 20-year-old from Hamilton who was rewriting the Canadian record book. It was Malar, not Limpert, who was pegged as Canada's best medal hope.

Limpert was miffed that she had allowed another swimmer to get past her, but in retrospect she says swimming in Malar's shadow freed her from intense public scrutiny and allowed her to focus. She was calm and relaxed as she stepped on the block for the 200-metre individual medley. Two minutes and 14.35 seconds later, she was Canada's swimming sweetheart and an Olympic silver medallist. Malar finished fourth.

There were suggestions Limpert's medal should have been gold because the winner, Ireland's Michelle Smith, was on steroids at the time but wasn't caught until later. The Canadian Olympic Association petitioned unsuccessfully to get Limpert the gold, but Limpert herself wasn't a fan of the effort. "I didn't want to get a gold like that. Ironically, if I had won, I'd probably have retired," she says. "I'm swimming faster now than I ever have, and I'm still having a lot of fun." Who'd have thought losing a gold medal would be a blessing?

Limpert's position as the backbone of the Canadian swim effort was buoyed by gold medals at the Commonwealth Games in Kuala Lumpur in 1998 and at the Pan American Games in Winnipeg in 1999. She competed in four events in the Sydney Games. While she recorded a personal best in the 200 individual medley, she failed to swim away with a medal.

But in the wake of criticism about the Canadians' overall lacklustre performance in Australia, she surfaced as a spokeswoman on athletic funding and training. "Strengthening amateur sport will benefit the health care system,

because fewer people will require medical care," she preaches to anyone who will listen. Daily gym classes in school are a must, she says, and athletic funding must be boosted to ease the burden on the families of promising young athletes who are looking at mountains of bills for training, travel, and equipment.

Hurt that some critics in her hometown have characterized her efforts on behalf of the next generation of swimmers as "whiny," she insists her motives are pure and that she would never do anything that would bring disrepute to her sport or her country. In fact, the patriotism instilled in her by her German-born parents is more than skin deep. In 1994, Limpert had a red Maple Leaf tattooed just above her right ankle just so people would know she was from Canada when swimming in exotic locales.

Her parents, Heinz and Marianne, deserve some of the credit for the dogged determination that has allowed Limpert to stay strokes ahead of the competition, long after many swimmers her age have hung up their goggles. Heinz was a German and Canadian amateur heavyweight boxing champion who made the 1964 Canadian Olympic team but wasn't eligible to compete because he hadn't lived in Canada long enough. He was unable to achieve his own Olympic dream but was in his daughter's corner every step of the way while she pursued and fulfilled hers. In a show of gratitude for his unwavering support, timely pep talks, and poolside cheering, she had her 1996 Olympic ring sized for his finger. Her mother, less vocal but equally supportive, now wears Limpert's Olympic ring from Sydney.

"Athletes have responsibilities to act responsibly because there are young kids watching what they do, but parents are the best role models," says Limpert. "I would never want to do anything that would make my parents ashamed of me." On the contrary, she does much beyond the pool to make her parents proud. She has been spokeswoman for the New Brunswick Arthritis Society and travelled with the Future is Female program, encouraging girls to pursue their dreams. She speaks at conferences encouraging people to exercise for fun and to make healthy choices and offers advice and support to young swimmers.

Limpert is especially proud that a scholarship in her name is presented annually at Fredericton High School, because she believes education is important. That point was underscored in December 2001, when after 10 years of trying to marry classes with international travel, she was thrilled to receive a bachelor of arts degree. "This isn't going in the drawers," she said with a laugh. "It

Olympic swimmer Marianne Limpert signs an autograph for six-year-old Anna Walker of Oromocto, New Brunswick, at a news conference at King's Place Mall in Fredericton, December 20, 2000. Limpert says she's going to keep on swimming, surprising many who assumed the 28-year-old was about to throw in the towel.

took me a while, but I didn't give up. I'm framing this thing, and it's going to be the first thing people see when they come into any house I own."

With her degree in hand and promising times in competition, Limpert's competitive fire still burns bright. A fourth Olympics in Athens, 2004, is a strong possibility, she says. When she has lingering doubts, she draws strength from the story of Wilma Rudolph, an American who overcame bouts of polio, double pneumonia, and scarlet fever to win triple gold in the 1960 Olympics.

This athlete supports:
Arthritis Society
National Office
393 University Avenue, Suite 1700
Toronto, ON M5G 1E6
website: www.arthritis.ca

Marnie McBean
Race Cadet

BORN: JANUARY 28, 1968
TORONTO, ONTARIO

It was just after the 1984 Olympics. Marnie McBean saw a commercial on TV for Coffee Crisp chocolate bars. It was a silly commercial, she says in hindsight, but it had rowing in it. Then she saw the movie Oxford Blues, in which a brash young American goes to prestigious Oxford University in England and ends up on the rowing team. "I came out thinking, Rob Lowe looks great in jeans, but how do you learn to row?" The 17-year-old got out the phone book and found the number for Toronto's Argonaut Rowing Club.

A couple of months later, she was taking lessons. McBean swam at the Memorial Pool from 8 until 10 every Saturday morning, then rode her bike 10 kilometres to the rowing club. "I loved it right from the start. I wasn't skilled right away, but it must have been something I took to very naturally." She was barely through the basic classes when a sports reporter for the Globe and Mail came up to her and said, "You're going to go really far, make the national team." One year later, McBean won bronze at the World Junior Rowing Championship. The next time she saw that reporter, McBean was competing at the 1992 Olympics in Barcelona.

At 5 feet 10 inches, the four-time Olympic medallist says she is a bit short for a sport where most athletes stand 6 feet. "But there was something in the sport I took to really quickly. I think it was more a sense that I had a feel for the water...You can teach someone to row, but it's a lot more difficult to teach them to be aggressive or to feel the water."

McBean didn't have to be taught that competitive edge; it was ingrained. She wanted to be the best in the world, both in speed and technique. Within five years, she was.

National rowing coach Brian Richardson ended up matching McBean with Kathleen Heddle. Talk about opposites! McBean is outgoing and tenacious, whereas Heddle is private and reserved. They really didn't want to compete together at first. "I kept trying to make Kathleen competitive," says McBean. "If I could find out what the right buttons to press were, then she'd be competitive and aggressive." McBean admits she overdid it as she tried to motivate Heddle to be like her.

Both McBean and Heddle felt they weren't a good match and asked to row with someone else. "She saw my quest to find the right button as nattering, and I was frustrated." But their coach insisted they work together. Once McBean put

Canada's Kathleen Heddle (left) and Marnie McBean (right) row their way to a gold medal in the women's double sculls event at the 1996 Atlanta Summer Olympic Games.

her preconceived notions aside, she started to see a side of Heddle she had missed before. She watched her train and compete and saw Heddle place first in every test they were put through. "Kathleen's performance was exceptional on the team. Everyone sort of looked at Silken [Laumann] and myself as being the best rowers of the '90s. It was Kathleen."

McBean came to see Heddle had commitment and passion for her sport; it just didn't bubble out as it did with herself: "I started realizing that the only way Kathleen could be so good was if she really was competitive and aggressive. And my nattering changed its focus and Kathleen realized I'm a perfectionist on the water and that all the verbal addressing I was doing was designed to get us working together. So she calmed down and started listening and paying attention to me, and I calmed down and stopped talking so much—and we started working better together."

The duo hit the international circuit in 1991 and set a world's best time when they won the World Championship, a record that went undefeated for seven years despite equipment changes that

111

made boats sleeker and faster. They won double gold at the Summer Olympics the next year, rowing together and as part of a team of eight. The very diversity that threatened to tear them apart at first made them the best pair in women's heavyweight rowing in the early 1990s.

When Heddle returned to school, McBean set out on her own and had just as much success. She took silver at the 1993 World Championships and gold in the quad sculls. The following year, she added the World Cup overall title to her list of accomplishments. McBean called up her friend and asked her if she wanted to team up again. They brought home silver from the World Championships in Indianapolis two months later and gold and silver the following year. As of 1997, McBean and Heddle were Canada's most decorated Summer Games Olympians.

McBean continued her solo career with such success that she became the first rower to win a medal in every event. She has won Olympic and World Championship medals in six different boats; each of them has had the word "fate" in its name. She was vying for a Canadian record fourth Olympic gold at the Sydney Games when she had to withdraw because of back trouble. This

was a devastating blow for McBean, who had returned to international competition from retirement.

McBean spent weeks—both before and after surgery for a protrusion on one of her spinal discs—flat on her back. In the end, she did make it to the Olympics—as a spectator. It was a humbling experience. "I made myself vulnerable," she says. Unable to sit and barely able to walk, McBean would lie on the patio floor of a coffee shop with a bag beneath her head and simply chat with fellow athletes, getting to know people she never would have had the pleasure of meeting as a focused and somewhat distant athlete bent on taking home yet another gold medal. Rather than lose a shot at a medal, McBean gained friendships she otherwise would never have.

The rower's final medal tally is impressive enough as it is: three Olympic gold and one bronze, eight World Championship medals, and 30 World Cup medals. McBean says the medals hold "no particular glow or excitement when I look at them." The joy she gets is the thrill on the face of a fan who holds one, and the memories of the races, the hard work, and the people who helped her along the way.

An inductee to the Canadian Sports Hall of Fame, McBean says she misses rowing terribly: "I miss the lifestyle of training. I miss being that good and being that capable and just having complete confidence." Now she fills her days and many evenings speaking at schools and corporations and working for numerous foundations, including the Kids Help Phone and Special Olympics. Believing that successful athletes should help others attain their goals, she founded a program called Fundraiser for Olympic Rowers Survival (FORS).

But her passion is working with children: "I like kids to know they should just try, try anything, try everything; that they can do anything." McBean doesn't see these numerous commitments as a drain on her time.

"It's about talking to people and it's about being kind and listening and receiving questions that I've been asked a thousand times like it's the first time I've been asked it."

Today is just like one of many in McBean's life these days. It's mid morning and she's sitting in a hotel restaurant sipping coffee. She was up late last night at a fundraiser for mentally challenged kids. As she slices into the cantaloupe on her plate, McBean says she thrives on her work, just as she used to thrive on the thrill of competition. She's now part of another hugely successful team. "For athletes, we're not the people giving the care, and we're not the people who are giving our time daily to one particular cause, but we're helping foundations raise the money that will allow the people to do what they do. I'm just so happy to be able to give back. I get to fill my time by giving back to a greater community that has taken care of me."

This athlete supports:
Kids Help Phone
(Chapters across Canada)
website: www.kidshelp.sympatico.ca

Jean-Luc Brassard
Flying High with Feet Firmly on the Ground

BORN: AUGUST 24, 1972
GRANDE-ILE, QUEBEC

When Olympic gold medallist Jean-Luc Brassard talks to schoolchildren about his experiences as one of the world's top freestyle skiers, he's always on the lookout for the shy boy or girl who gets pushed to the back of the group. Growing up in rural Quebec, he was always the student at the back, Brassard says. He remembers dreaming endlessly about shaking hands with some big-name athlete and how he would be able to retell that story over and over to his parents and his friends. But because he was shy and because few athletes ventured to Grande-Ile, 30 kilometres south of Montreal, that dream went unfulfilled.

Now, two decades later, with three World Cup moguls championships and an Olympic gold medal to his credit, Brassard, 30, is doing his best to ensure the early dreams of young Canadians aren't dashed too. "If I can give them a thrill, that's great. If I can inspire them to pursue their own dream, that's even better." Brassard has made the trek through classrooms in Quebec and Ontario every April for the past nine years. He goes to almost every school that requests a visit and doesn't ask for anything in return, not even gas money. Watching the handsome, ever-smiling veteran of the nation's freestyle skiing team laughing and joking with the kids, it's easy to underestimate his fierce competitor's spirit.

Certainly, many of his rivals have, and as a result, they were left eating snow. In competition, Brassard bobs and bounces through a 250-metre layout of bumps, mashing moguls, his knees working like shock absorbers in a finely tuned sports car, making the ride look smooth and graceful. Twice during the run, he jumps wildly into the air, soaring like an eagle and then twisting to perform heart-stopping moves one might think only possible on a trampoline. So innovative and imitated is his style, that one jump has been named after him: the JLB.

He's not the fastest mogul skier in the world, but Brassard compensates with fluid motions and an original style that has led him to achieve almost every conceivable success in the sport, including 40 World Cup medals and an Olympic gold in 1994. But even after winning all his medals, which are proudly displayed in a corner of the family home in Grande-Ile, and enduring the heartbreak of failing to reach the final at his final Olympics in Salt Lake City, he says his competitive pulse still beats strong. "There is still the thrill of going somewhere I haven't been before," he says, "to see how deep you can reach inside yourself to achieve your dreams."

The philosophy does not apply just on the mountainside. It applies to life and helps explain how his curiosity often leads him into discussions with mechanics and lift operators about the way things work. It also explains why he jumped at the chance last year to host a series of 30-minute programs on Quebec television unravelling the science of everyday items.

It may also account for his decision to try his hand at rap music in the 2000 hip-hop video, "Take Control," sponsored by BF Goodrich as a fundraiser for young freestyle skiers who have talent but few resources. Brassard saw it as a good cause and something he hadn't tried before. So he drafted teammates Nicholas Fontaine, Jennifer Heil, and Jennifer Simm to perform. "I'm no singer, but I've seen too many potential champions quitting freestyle for lack of funding. Doing the song was one way I could help them." Not everyone

Jean-Luc Brassard, of Grand-Ile, Quebec, performs his trademark cossack jump during an honorary run before the final moguls event at the XIX Olympic Winter Games in Deer Valley, Utah, February 12, 2002. Brassard failed to qualify for the finals in what will probably be his last Olympics.

appreciated the finer points of the effort—certainly no one has offered him a record deal—but it did generate interest in his sport and garnered a $31,500 donation from BF Goodrich.

Brassard is not a big man. At five feet seven inches, he may even look small on the slopes, but he is a giant when giving back to the community, especially if it involves kids. For the past four years, he has been the official spokesperson for Operation Enfant Soleil, a group dedicated to raising money for child health services in Quebec. As part of his responsibilities, he participates in a 24-hour telethon and spearheads a 15-day tour, visiting children in hospitals throughout Quebec. "Seeing the faces of young children light up when I visit them in the hospital is every bit as rewarding as placing first at an event," he says. "I have learned a lot about courage from them."

When he gets upset after a bad race or when something trivial blackens his mood, he conjures up the image of one of the many terminally ill kids he's encountered who remained smiling until the end. "It puts it all into perspective. When someone has to have their blood changed three times a week or has to live with tubes implanted in their body, my own problems become very small. These children are the real heroes. I feel privileged to get to know them."

The telethon raised $8 million in 2001, but Brassard wants no credit for the effort. He believes everyone has a role to play in society. He doesn't have the talent to be a surgeon and save lives, but he has the profile to help raise money, so he does. An avid golfer, Brassard also hosts an annual charity golf tournament in his hometown, with the proceeds going to the Optimist Club to build playgrounds, skateboard parks, and basketball courts for local kids.

In recognition of his outstanding athletic ability and his commitment to the community and charities in Quebec, he received, in March 2000, the Gillette World Champion Award. The prize came with a $50,000 cheque, which he promptly divided among the charities he supports. "This ranks right up there with the all the other world titles and gold medals," he said at the time. "It's a great feeling to know that not only have I touched people's lives through my skiing, but also through my charity work . . . I try to support different projects so children will have an opportunity to discover different sides of themselves," he says. "Inside every kid, therc is a treasure, a natural talent that just has to be developed."

Brassard discovered his own natural talent at age seven, shortly after he strapped on his first pair of skis. Surprisingly, he didn't enjoy traditional skiing; he found it boring. It wasn't until he found the bumps and began to "take air" that the passion revealed itself. Entering his first competition at age 13, he developed rapidly, joining the national team at age 17. The following year, he became the youngest skier to ever win the World Cup.

Brassard fought hard to have moguls embraced as a full-medal sport at the Olympics in 1992 and then captured hearts of millions in 1994 when he won Olympic gold at Lillehammer, Norway. With his skill, his smile, and his sense of humour revealed to the world, he quickly became the down-to-earth global ambassador for freestyle. To this day, he is a cult hero in Japan.

At home, the victory was a huge boost to the sport and prompted the establishment of the Canadian Freestyle Ski Association. There are now more than 50 active freestyle clubs in Canada. His talents are recognized not only by loyal fans. In recognition of his sportsmanship, conduct, and ability on the international scene, he has been presented the John Semmelink Award three times. The award is the highest honour the sport can bestow on one of its own.

But with the profile came high expectations for a stellar performance at the 1998 Olympics in Nagano, Japan. It didn't happen. Finishing fourth, Brassard

Former world champion and Olympic gold medallist Jean-Luc Brassard holds up a copy of a new CD he made with other skiers to help raise funds for the ski team, during a news conference in Montreal, October 17, 2000.

says he put too much pressure on himself. Worse still, he made some ill-advised comments about how the responsibility of being the Canadian flag-bearer at the opening ceremonies had hurt his performance and how too little French was spoken in the athletes' village. His remarks were seen as anti-Canadian, something he vehemently denies.

But the criticism and the frustration of finishing out of the medals ate away at him. Ironically, it was only when he was forced to the sidelines after tearing up his knee at a World Cup event in March 2000 that he was able get back in winning form. "I realized I was trying to be what some people wanted me to be, not who I am. I'm still hard on myself, I still try to do better than the race before, but if I do my best and I don't win, I don't beat myself up over it."

That was the attitude he took to the Salt Lake City Olympics and, as he dominated the training sessions, it looked as though it would be enough to take him to the podium one more time. But he faltered during the actual competition. He went for broke, trying two of the most difficult tricks attempted among the 30 skiers, but landed awkwardly both times, and ended up finishing 21st. It was not the way he had envisioned the end to his Olympic career.

But even as tears of disappointment flowed down his cheeks, he didn't make excuses. He didn't blame the knee. He didn't blame the pressure. Instead, he tried to find a bright spot in the wreckage of his Olympic dream. "This is a big disappointment, but when you put yourself in front of people, you have to accept what happens. Some 14 months ago they were teaching me to walk again. I didn't get the medal, but I was at least able to ski in the Olympics."

This athlete supports:

Opération Enfant Soleil

2160 rue Jean-Talon Nord, Office 200

Sainte-Foy, QC G1N 2G3

website: www.oes@oes.qc.ca

Myriam Bedard
Good Aim, Great Heart

BORN: DECEMBER 22, 1969
ANCIENNE LORETTE, QUEBEC

When Myriam Bedard was 15 years old, three fellow cadets asked her to be the fourth member of their biathlon team for a local competition. They had to have a woman on the team and they knew Bedard was an excellent shot and in great physical shape. She accepted and, with a rifle slung over her shoulders, borrowed skis, and oversized boots stuffed with Kleenex, Bedard started down the path that would lead her to become the world's best female biathlete.

The team didn't win that day, but Bedard had discovered her passion. Within two years, she was the Canadian junior champion and she would go on to write Olympic history by winning gold in both the 7.5-kilometre and 15-kilometre biathlon events at Lillehammer, Norway, in 1994.

Biathlon is the least recognized and most challenging of all the winter Olympic sports. It involves cross-country skiing for 30 to 60 minutes along 7.5 kilometres or 15 kilometres of twisting track, stopping at specific intervals to shoot 10 or 20 targets. Former U.S. biathlete Don Neilson once described it as "sprinting full out around the neighbourhood track and then stopping to thread a needle."

By the time she was 28, Bedard was the best at this kind of needlework. Pretty ironic for someone who preferred figure skating to skiing as a kid. "It was too hard," she recalls. But she was a fierce competitor with a crack shot and nerves of steel. Many Olympic biathletes miss valuable shots, she says, because they can't handle the stress. They can't calm down enough for a steady shot. Bedard says she had the balance, endurance, and drive to win from the beginning; all she needed was to learn how to cross-country ski.

She learned quickly, joining the national junior team at 17 and winning her first senior championship the next year. In her second year on the Canadian senior team, Bedard gained international respect, finishing second in the 1990–1 World Cup standings. More victories followed. She became the first North American to win an Olympic medal in biathlon when she claimed a bronze at the 1992 Games in Albertville. She was named world champion in 1993, then took the ultimate—double gold at the 1994 Olympics in Lillehammer. That made her not only the first Canadian woman to win two Olympic gold medals but also the first North American athlete to win gold in the biathlon.

Bedard says she has the cadets to thank for much of her success. As an active teen always seeking adventure, she says cadets filled her free weekends with loads of challenges. "I think teenagers need to be very busy, have activities outside of school. I was a teen who was very interested in life and enjoyed a lot of challenges and becoming a leader." She spent time on survival courses in the woods and was selected to go to the Arctic Circle to spend six weeks with the Inuit on Baffin Island.

Not surprisingly, Bedard excelled as a cadet, being named Top Female Cadet and awarded the prestigious Duke of Edinburgh's gold level award in 1986. The same zest for life and challenge she exhibited as a cadet helped her become the best biathlete in the world. She recalls running and biking alone for hours by herself, regretting the missed sack time but aware that one doesn't become the best in the world at anything by lounging in bed.

Today, when Bedard speaks to schoolchildren about her athletic accomplishments, she's often asked what it's like to stand on the Olympic podium. What she'd rather talk about is the effort it

Canada's Myriam Bedard competing in the biathlon event at the 1992 Albertville Olympic Winter Games.

takes to get there. "It's hard work. Everybody has to work hard, even the best in the world. You can be the champion one day, and the next everybody is trying to beat you again. You have to work, work, work. Pick up your skis, set them in the track, and work."

To underscore the point, Bedard talks about her triumph in Norway. She was a favourite and had trained hard to get there, but did badly in her first race. She hadn't slept well and the crowd of spectators was rowdy. But she forced herself to tune out those distractions and concentrate on the task at hand. She won by almost 30 seconds, giving her a victory that still means everything to her. "I felt that this was the last time that this could ever happen to me; it's so exceptional in the biathlon, so I appreciated it; it was a very special moment." She was wrong. A few days later, she took gold again in the 7.5-kilometre race.

Despite the effort it took to get them, Bedard's medals aren't proudly displayed in a living room cabinet. They're safely stowed away in the bank. They're more like museum pieces, she says, representing a moment in her life but not defining who she is. "They're not a part of me," she says, though she

admits, "they're very special to look at."

After her success in Lillehammer, Bedard married fellow biathlete Jean Paquet. She announced in 1994 that not only was she going to have a baby but that she was going to compete again the following year. Everything seemed to be going Bedard's way. But halfway through 1995 she fell ill. She was constantly exhausted. Tests eventually told her she had hypothyroidism, a condition that slows the metabolism, as well as chronic fatigue syndrome. On top of that, she developed allergies to foods that were crucial sources of energy to her as an athlete, foods such as dairy products and bananas.

So how does one reach performance level, let alone be a mother, after those diagnoses? It's a question she still asks herself. "Before I got pregnant I promised myself that I would compete again. I need to be an athlete . . . It's good that I did make that promise because otherwise you could just stay home and cry about your sickness." Bedard saw a lot of doctors and worked hard to find the right dosage of medication for her high-performance lifestyle.

After three years of dogged determination, driven by her formidable will, Bedard re-entered international

123

Myriam Bedard and her daughter, Maude, walk to the finish line for the last time in active competition. Bedard participated in the biathlon World Cup at the Centre de Biathlon Myriam-Bedard, Valcartier, north of Quebec City, March 5, 1999.

competition at the 1998 Winter Olympics in Nagano, Japan. But it was not to be the comeback she dreamed of. The snow was in bad shape and the wax she was using to make her skis slide better just wasn't working. The race was a struggle for everyone. Never in her entire life did she suffer so much.

"It was sad, because I was in very, very good shape. I could not believe my career could end on a sad note like that." Journalists from around the world were there to witness her comeback. Hundreds of thousands of Canadians were glued to their TV sets, looking to her to earn a medal for their country. Bedard placed 32nd in the 7.5-kilometre race and 50th in the 15-kilometre, but Bedard wasn't disappointed in herself. Far from it; she had made a tremendous comeback just by being there. "I did nothing wrong, I did the best I could and the best thing I did was finish the race."

Even that was a feat in itself. The last

kilometre of the race was all uphill. As she headed into the grade, she passed the wax room. It would have been so easy to slide in there, put on a fresh coat and head back out, but she knew that it would take too long, that the race would be over before she herself reached the finish line if she stopped. Her competitive drive kicked in: "I have to finish, I have people waiting for me at the finish line," she told herself.

After that race, at age 28, Bedard announced her retirement. She remains committed, however, to speaking up for all sport has done for her. In 2001, she was named to the Olympic Order for her outstanding personal achievements and contributions to the sport. Though she has a day job with the marketing department at Via Rail, she continues to deliver motivational speeches to schools and business. Bedard didn't win a medal that day—she didn't even place. But for her, the victory rested in just being there. As she told *Time* magazine, "I didn't quit, and that showed me something about myself."

The All-Stars

Trevor Linden
Caring for Kids

BORN: APRIL 11, 1970
MEDICINE HAT, ALBERTA

He was so proud of that car. Trevor Linden had worked since he was 11 years old, picking up golf balls at the local range and washing golf clubs, earning the money that would buy him his first car five years later. It was a 1972 silver Datsun 240Z. "I was the most proud guy in Medicine Hat, driving around in that car."

Today, as a star centre with the Vancouver Canucks, Linden could buy that car many times over with his $4 million a year salary. But thanks to his upbringing, he has never forgotten the value of a dollar. Parents Edna and Lane were small-business owners who had worked hard all their lives. They expected the same of their three sons. "I know how hard you had to work to buy that 10-speed bike, or that car at age 16. I learned the value of a dollar early in life and I respect how hard people work," says Linden.

Linden spent hours at the family farm outside Medicine Hat, picking rocks or sweeping out the granaries. "The biggest thing [our parents] taught us was to take care of ourselves; to work hard. If you work hard, you can achieve anything you want. I'm just so thankful for the parents I had." That determination carried over into his hockey playing

later in life. "My game was always built around hard work. I never considered myself loaded with talent. My game is structured around hard work and skill."

Dad Lane Linden agrees. He once said, "Trevor was never a standout on any of the teams he played with. There were always two or three kids who were as good or better than Trev. But Trevor had a determination that was unparalleled." That unwavering persistence made Linden the youngest player in the NHL the season he was drafted, the youngest member of an all-star team, the NHL's youngest captain at just 21, and a World Cup champion.

Like most Canadian kids shooting pucks at local rinks, Linden dreamed of playing in the NHL. At six feet four inches and 211 pounds, his physique helped. But Linden is known for being a tough player with tremendous leadership qualities. He has spent most of his career with the Canucks, though he had brief stints with the Montreal Canadiens, New York Islanders and, most recently, the Washington Capitols. He's thrilled to be back in Canada. "I never wanted to leave." What did he miss most about home while he was in the States? *Hockey Night in Canada,* of course.

Linden first became a hometown

Trevor Linden in action at the 1998 Nagano Winter Olympics in Japan.

hero as a junior player with the Medicine Hat Tigers, leading the team to two WHL championships and back-to-back Memorial Cup Championships. Linden helped Canada win gold at the 1988 World Junior Championships and, in 1991, was a silver medallist for Canada at the World Championships. He played for Canada again at the World Cup in 1996, winning silver. He went on to play for Canada at both the Winter Olympics and World Championships two years later.

In 1989, Linden was drafted by the Canucks, scoring his first goal in October and earning a place on the all-rookie team. When the 1993–4 season swung around, he led the Canucks to the Stanley Cup finals and eventually earned the Iron Man title for playing 482 consecutive games over six years. He has been recognized for his tremendous on-ice success, winning the Molson Cup four times and twice winning trophies for being the Canucks' leading scorer and Most Exciting Player.

But Linden is most admired for his off-ice triumphs. Deeply committed to helping people, in 1997 Linden was awarded the King Clancy Trophy—a prestigious NHL award for leadership both on and off the ice—for his humanitarian efforts. He also received the Gillette World Champion Award as the Canadian athlete who best exemplifies excellence in sports, as well as compassion and humanitarianism in the community. Linden visits terminally ill children at British Columbia Children's Hospital and works with a hospice for terminally ill children and their families.

Linden is so concerned about young people that he spearheaded his own community program, Captain's Crew. It enables underprivileged kids to go to Canucks games for free. They get to enjoy their own luxury suite, a trip in a limousine and, best of all, a visit with Linden. His reward for doing this, says Linden, is having these children know people care about them.

Linden even hand-cycled 60 kilometres across the interior of B.C. in a wheelchair to help a friend who was paralyzed in a car accident. John Ryan was hand-cycling across Canada to raise money for spinal cord research, and Linden said his friend was such an inspiration, he wanted to help. So he did it the way he knows best: he got out there and did it himself. "I'm so proud of how he handles being a hockey player, and

probably more so what he does in the community with charities—and with kids especially," says Ryan.

At one point, Linden got involved in so many charities for the underprivileged, handicapped, and terminally ill that he formed an umbrella group, the Trevor Linden Foundation, to coordinate his efforts. "What you see with Trevor is what you get," said his mother. "He's an honourable, honest young man who is committed to helping out kids. He feels he has to make a difference and that's what motivates him. He doesn't care about any publicity."

Some people just sign a cheque and never see the ones they help. Not Linden. He wants to spend time with the kids. "It's something I truly enjoy doing," he says, embarrassed by the attention his efforts draw. "I just prefer to do it privately." Besides, he realizes he is an important role model: "I feel fortunate to be in the position that I can make a difference with my time, that I can really make a difference in young people's lives."

It takes a special person to be able to sit with a child dying of cancer. But Linden says he does it to bring a few carefree moments into their often-daunting lives. "I want them to just

Trevor Linden of the Vancouver Canucks poses with the King Clancy Memorial Trophy after winning it at the NHL Awards in Toronto.

have fun, to take their minds off things." So much of the children's time is focused on white blood counts, plasma levels, and doctors' reports. Linden wants them to talk about their hobbies, last night's hockey game, their hometowns, "just stuff."

When he first started working with sick children, he thought it would be intimidating. But, he says, "when you see how strong these young kids are and the fearlessness and determination, it's amazing. And it gives strength to you. You're trying to help them but they give it back." He's so inspired by his time with these youngsters that he looks forward to the day he and his wife Cristina will share that joy with their own children.

This athlete supports:
Trevor Linden Foundation
PO Box 29175
Delamont Postal Outlet
Vancouver, BC V6J 5C7

Lorie Kane
Able Kane

BORN: DECEMBER 19, 1964
CHARLOTTETOWN, PRINCE EDWARD ISLAND

When Lorie Kane won her first tournament in the summer of 2000, it wasn't just her caddy who showered her with celebratory beer. Many of her rivals on the LPGA tour had changed plane tickets and rearranged reservations just so they could be on hand in St. Louis when the popular Prince Edward Island golfer finally snagged her first professional victory.

After four seasons of heart-breaking misses and nine second-place career finishes, the trip to the winner's circle at the Michelob Light Classic was a mixture of joy and relief for both Kane and the pros who came to admire her. Perhaps most importantly, the victory—combined with two other late-season wins—put to rest nagging doubts about whether the nicest player on the tour had the tools to also be one of the best. "I'm glad my first win was a beer tournament," says Kane in an interview from the Florida condominium she uses when she's not at home in Charlottetown. "The image of me standing there, doused in beer, laughing. It really puts everything in perspective. It says everything about who I am and what I'm doing."

That doesn't mean the best Canadian female golfer in a decade can't sip champagne and mingle with the elite at the fanciest tour galas. "She can hold her own in any situation, but she's just such a down-to-earth girl that at a multi-course meal, she'd be more worried about the burden on the kitchen staff than what was being served or who was being honoured," says Kent Hudson, a long-time friend and chairperson of Kane's annual charity golf tournament.

"She's charismatic without trying," agrees Dave MacNeil, executive director of Sport P.E.I. and the former basketball coach Kane credits with encouraging her to go after her dream of joining the ladies' tour. "Travelling and meeting all kinds of celebrities, it would be easy to get caught up in it all. But not Lorie. She's never lost sight of people who helped her out, both locally and on tour. She will routinely go into the kitchen at the big tournaments to make sure she's thanked all the volunteers who make tournaments work."

Kane is equally gracious with fans. She arrives early and stays late at many events, signing autographs and allowing her picture to be taken with golf enthusiasts from Moosejaw to the Maritimes. Her bright, lottery-winner smile always accompanies her.

If there has been one thing that has

earned her criticism, it's her traditional Canadian willingness to accommodate people. Some pundits have suggested that her Girl Scout-like compulsion to please gets in the way of her ability to perform. The criticism irks her. "I'm a very competitive individual, but I don't want to win at any cost. I'm not going to bad-mouth anyone, or play mind games that will make someone else feel bad. Some people say in competition you check your friendship at the door and pick it up again at the end of the day, but I don't believe that. Golf is a game of honour and I love playing it. You don't have to be a killer to win. Look at Wayne Gretzky. He's the best hockey player there's ever been, and he's a nice guy on and off the ice. I don't think anyone can be too nice."

Hockey talk peppers any conversation with Kane. Her passion for the stick and puck rivals her interest in golf. She's an ardent Toronto Maple Leafs and Montreal Canadiens fan, and credits the television coverage of Mark Messier's return to the New York Rangers with helping her to focus just prior to her first win.

And win she has. The 37-year-old has won four pro tournaments, scooted past the $3-million mark in total win-nings, and ranked fourth overall in 2001 on the ladies' pro circuit. Arguably the most famous islander since fictional heroine Anne of Green Gables, Kane is a two-time winner of the Bobbie Rosenfeld Award as Canada's female athlete of the year (1997 and 2000), and was runner-up for the award in both 1998 and 2001. In 1998, she won the Heather Farr Player award, given to the LPGA player who demonstrates dedication and love of the game while fulfilling her goals as a player. In 2000, Kane received the William and Mousie Powell Award, which recognized her as the peer-selected player most exemplifying the spirit, ideals, and values of the Association.

But even with those top awards in hand—and on display at her parents' Charlottetown home—Kane still finds it hard to believe she is playing with the elite golfers of the world. "I pinch myself sometimes, thinking, 'I'm going to wake up and it's going to be all over.'"

As a teen, Kane was a "typical jock." She played basketball and field hockey, tried gymnastics, and even took a stab at synchronized swimming. She started playing golf at age five under the watchful eye of her father, Jack, a local pro, but didn't enter a tournament until she was

Lorie Kane hits her second shot on the 15th fairway during the LPGA Du Maurier Gold Classic in Aylmer, Quebec, August 12, 2000. Kane finished the day tied with Annika Sorenstam at 6-under-par.

13. She worked summers at the pro shop, first cleaning clubs in the back, and then, as she grew older, selling golf gear out front, and talking endlessly with weekend duffers about clubs, lies, techniques, and hazards.

A borderline-C student in high school, she relied on her skills outside the classroom to give her the confidence she needed to become the success she is today. It is perhaps one reason she is such a big supporter of KidSport, a national program that pays up to $200 in membership fees for young people who don't have the money to join local teams. The program runs in several provinces, but Kane is the largest single supporter of the island's branch. "I always believe there is going to be someone there to take care of the sick kids. I'm trying to reach the kids who fall through the cracks, but might make it, if they can only get a positive start," she explains.

Before turning professional in 1993, Kane enjoyed a successful amateur career. She was a member of the Canadian International team from 1989 to 1992, of the Canadian Commonwealth team in 1991, and of the 1992 Canadian World Amateur team. She still carries a divot tool in her golf bag that she picked up at the Worlds.

While urging young golfers to follow their dreams, she uses examples from her career to remind them that nothing comes without sacrifice and setbacks. As an amateur, she once had to sue a golf association after "backroom politics," not rules or ability, left her off

Korean golfer Se Ri Pak (left) is congratulated by Lorie Kane after sinking a putt worth $72,500 during the Lorie Kane Island Challenge at the Brudenell Golf Course in Roseneath, Prince Edward Island, on August 30, 2000. Kane hosted the two-day event, which also featured Annika Sorenstam of Sweden and Nancy Lopez of the United States.

the national team for an important event. She won the lawsuit and played well in the tournament. "It wasn't something she wanted to do," recalls her sister Mary Lynn Jenkins, a lawyer who looks after Kane's business affairs. "But it was about fairness. The association thought she was going to roll over, but she stood her ground. It took a lot of courage."

It took her three tries to get her full-time LPGA qualifying card, Kane reveals. Then it was four years of exhausting fundraising and part-time play before

she was able to join the tour as a full-time member in 1997. "The first couple of years, I helped to raise the funds I needed. I think it was good for me to do that because it taught me to have faith in myself. The hardest thing to sell is yourself."

Kane now plays 25 to 30 tournaments a year and has her sights on becoming number one. "I don't want to be a player who has won a tournament or four. The knife isn't even halfway into the cake with that. I know I can be the

138

best, maybe even end up in the Hall of Fame." Her agenda may be heavy, but she still makes time to help the next generation of golfers. South Korean golfer Se Ri Pak calls Kane "her angel" because of the way Kane helped her adjust to Western culture.

Others call Kane an angel for the time and money she offers to charity. Since 1998, the Lorie Kane Golf Classic has been held annually at the Belvedere Golf Club in Charlottetown and has raised $300,000 for Ronald McDonald Children's Charities of Canada. The money has been used to help support Ronald McDonald House in Halifax, purchase specialized equipment for the Rehabilitation Room at the Queen Elizabeth Hospital in Charlottetown, and pay for children with severe learning disabilities to visit the P.E.I. Snoezelen Room, a special room where their senses are stimulated by music, lighting effects, and gentle vibrations.

Unlike some charity events, where athletes simply lend their names to the event, Kane is an active participant at the Lorie Kane Golf Classic. She plays at least one hole with every foursome, talking with them and sharing tips and tour stories. Hudson said that after dinner, Kane won't leave the room until she's talked with everyone in attendance. "At the end of the day, there's 150 people who can truthfully boast that they've played golf with Canada's finest," he says.

There's one coin Kane won't be donating to charity or spending on the junk food she loves but is trying to cut back on. It's a 1989 lucky loonie, kissed on either side by her nieces, Charlotte and Marcie. She uses it as a ball marker, and it serves as a reminder that no matter where she travels, she has her family and a nation full of fans rooting for her.

This athlete supports:

K i d S p o r t   F u n d
c/o Sport PEI
PO Box 302
Charlottetown, PEI C1A 7K7

R o n a l d   M c D o n a l d   C h i l d r e n ' s
C h a r i t i e s   o f   C a n a d a
McDonald's Place
Toronto, ON M3C 3L4
e-mail: rmcc@mcdonalds.ca

Todd MacCulloch
Full Court Impressive

BORN: JANUARY 27, 1976
WINNIPEG, MANITOBA

When Todd MacCulloch was in elementary school, he thought he had the coolest dad of all the kids in the class. At show and tell, Todd would sit at his desk, proudly grinning as Sandy MacCulloch showed the class photographs of the airplane he flew and unfolded his red serge RCMP uniform. The National Basketball Association star says he didn't idolize athletes growing up. "But I had a great role model: my father. He taught me about life, about how to treat people. I try to model my life after his."

The New Jersey Nets centre with a six-year, $34-million contact now imparts those values to schoolchildren across North America. He loves to talk to them about the value of an education, the importance of literacy, the dangers of drugs, and his faith in God. Big-name athletes have a responsibility to give back to society, he says. "You can do as little as you want or as much as you want, and I'm grateful that I'm part of an organization that gives me a lot of opportunity to do things, to speak to kids." He tells the children that, "No matter what the odds are against you, you can be successful if you set the right priorities first. I never had the NBA as a priority. I knew it was important to graduate from high school and that basketball was secondary."

College was paid for thanks to a basketball scholarship, but MacCulloch says getting a degree was still his top priority. That way, no matter what happened with his basketball career, he had a well-rounded education that would get him a good job. "High school is just not good enough today; you have to have a degree." So MacCulloch took speech and hearing science at the University of Washington. If he ever uses his degree, he plans to head back to university for a master's degree so that he can work with children who have stuttering or hearing problems.

It was while he was studying in Washington that he met wife, Jana. She was taking a psychology degree, so she was "always trying to figure [him] out." He praises her for her selfless commitment to him, particularly in those early years, when the NBA was never a sure bet. "She was so influential, she allowed me to stay focused; she helped me feel better after my losses . . . She gave me peace of mind."

Seven feet tall by grade 12, was there ever any question that Todd MacCulloch would play basketball? "I don't think it was in the cards from the beginning," he

Canada's men's basketball team (clockwise from top left): head coach Jay Triano, Rowan Barrett, Greg Newton, Pete Guarsci, Todd MacCulloch, Michael Meeks, Eric Hinrichsen, Andrew Mavis, Sherman Hamilton, Steve Nash, Shawn Swords, David Daniels, and Greg Francis at the 2000 Sydney Olympic Games.

says. He didn't even start playing until he was 10 years old. By then, many of his American teammates and competitors in the United States had been on the court for years.

Hockey was the natural sport for a Canadian kid to take up. By the time MacCulloch was in kindergarten, he was at the rink as well. He played hockey for six years, but gave it up when he turned 11. "It was a bit too rigorous; I wanted to do something a bit more recreational, and basketball just fit me. I was a tall kid." He admits some adults in

his life pushed him towards the basketball court, but in the end he didn't need much persuading. His best friends loved the sport and they'd often hang out at the court for hours.

But MacCulloch never lost his love for hockey, so he was thrilled when years later he was playing for the Philadelphia 76ers and was offered a chance to play with the Flyers, just for fun. He borrowed his dad's size-13 skates, but just couldn't squeeze his size-19 feet into them. Unwilling to see the opportunity pass, MacCulloch's teammates surprised him by finding a sport store in Winnipeg that got the biggest pair of skates it could find and stretched them to fit.

MacCulloch was thrilled with them, but a scheduling conflict meant he missed his one shot to hit the ice with the Flyers. "It was a bit of a childhood dream." But there aren't too many dreams MacCulloch hasn't made come true. He's one of just four Canadians to make the NBA in the 2001–2 season and one of only 16 in the nation's history. A committed Canadian at heart, MacCulloch was reluctant to move to the United States, but recognized that if he were going to test himself against the best in basketball, that's where he'd have to go.

After a standout college career at the University of Washington, he was drafted by the 76ers in the second round of the 1999 NBA Draft. He took part in his first NBA all-star competition in 2000 and was selected to play with the 2000 Rookie team. Not surprisingly, he was a member of Team Canada at the 2000 Sydney Olympics. As a veteran centre for the Canadian Men's National Basketball team, MacCulloch helped lead the squad to a bronze-medal finish at the 2001 Tournament of the Americas in Argentina. That medal landed Canada a solid berth at the 2002 World Championships in Indianapolis. Back with the 76ers, he played two seasons as backup centre and made it into 23 playoff games.

MacCulloch became a free agent in August 2001 and was immediately snapped up by the Nets and subsequently had his breakout season for one of the Eastern Conference's hottest teams. After signing on MacCulloch, Nets' president Rod Thorn said of the Canadian, "[he] possesses soft hands and good footwork for a big man, and we feel that he will add size and skill to our centre."

He went from being a reserve player to starter right away, and MacCulloch says he's loving every minute of the game. The Nets have some of the league's best players, but he says their success in 2002 lay as much in their ability to work together as in their skills, and that has allowed the Nets to battle for the league championship.

The 76ers went to the finals the year MacCulloch was with them, and the Nets had an outstanding year with him on their club. But MacCulloch is too modest to take credit for the success: "I'm just a cog in the big machine. I'm just a contributor on my team . . . I'm a

Philadelphia 76ers players stand with the flags of the countries where they were born before the start of the Toronto Raptors game November 1, 2000, in Philadelphia. From left: Ademola Okulagja, Germany; Todd MacCulloch, Canada; Toni Kukoc, Croatia; and Pepe Shanchez, Argentina.

very imperfect player. Some of the other players have skills that I don't have." He says people like former Canadian National teammate Steve Nash of Victoria, B.C., now a star with the Dallas Mavericks, and Nets teammate Jason Kidd "deserve credit for being far bigger cogs in the wheel."

Besides getting more play time and the larger salary that comes with being a starter, MacCulloch says there's another advantage to playing with the Nets. He gets to wear the number 11. That's what he wore on his hockey jersey when his dad coached him as a youngster. And it's the number his dad wore when he played men's league. This is his way of saying thanks. "My dad has supported me throughout life." He

didn't know much about basketball until his son took it up, never having had much interest in it. But once his son started playing, Sandy MacCulloch gave him his full support and became Todd's number-one fan.

Todd MacCulloch says he will never forget either his family or his Canadian roots.

"I make it very clear to [my teammates] that I'm Canadian—I love Canada." He's always joking with them over Canadianisms such as "eh," and he comes home every chance he gets. "And whenever I get my feet on Canadian soil, I look for a 7-Eleven." It seems those Americans just don't know how to make a slurpee right.

Dave Rodney
An Everest Education

Born: June 27, 1964
Mankota, Saskatchewan

The most influential teacher in Dave Rodney's life stands 29,035 feet tall. Her name is Everest, and the 38-year-old speaker-filmmaker-educator from the flatlands of Saskatchewan has been drawn to her majesty three times. Undeterred by a broken back and a knee that has required four operations, Rodney has reached her summit twice: the only Canadian to get a repeat of the stunning view from the top of the world.

"It's the closest point a person can be to outer space and still have their feet on the ground," he says, sipping coffee in his Calgary home, sorting through expedition slides and neatly arranged stacks of videotape that have been featured in numerous documentaries. Pausing to study the image of a fellow climber peer over his oxygen mask at the vast panorama below, Rodney says his visits to the highest peak on the planet stretched his physical, spiritual, and psychological limits.

"The mountain does not care if you have a master's degree, possess an incredible résumé, or have the faith of a saint. On the mountain, you are on your own to fight your demons." One of Rodney's first lessons was that the challenges that really matter are the ones that happen at sea level, with the people all around us. That feeling was clearest in May 2001 when he stood on the top of the world for the second time. Gazing in wonder at the curvature of the Earth bending on every horizon, he became acutely aware how the peace and serenity of a Tibetan sunrise stood in stark contrast to the despair and anger of the world's dispossessed. The difference, he concluded, is how people play the hand they are dealt.

"When I experienced oxygen, equipment, and health complications during the climb, I had no one to turn to but myself. Good intentions don't get anyone to the top—on a mountain, at home, or in the corporate world. To a great extent, our attitude determines our altitude."

Treating the summit revelations as gifts bestowed upon him by the ancient mountain, Rodney shares his "Everest education" as a professional speaker and active charity fundraiser, encouraging and empowering people to tackle their "every-day Everests." Rodney takes the commitment to serve as an ambassador for his country and his sport seriously. In the last five years, he's shared the secrets of his success with students at more than 200 schools and 500 corporations, associations, and nonprofit organizations.

As part of his effort to put the "fun" back into fundraising, he has climbed on a step-mill for 16 hours straight for the Juvenile Diabetes Association and is listed in the *Guinness Book of Records* for topping off the world's largest freestanding canned food display. That effort netted the Calgary Inter-Faith Food Bank 11,075 cans of beans from an "indoor Everest" built by the people of Calgary. As a member of numerous education and civic committees, Rodney is especially pleased to do work with the Mustard Seed Street Ministry, a nonprofit, humanitarian organization providing food, shelter, education, and employment for the homeless.

Rodney has felt the call to climb since childhood. As a youngster, he recalls gazing at a painting of the Swiss Alps that hung in his grandfather's home in Avonlea, Saskatchewan, and wondering what the view would be like from the top of the mountain. As a youth, he was drawn to the mountains on hiking and skiing trips, and a passing interest in mountaineering blossomed into passion when he spent a year as a missionary educator on the island of St. Vincent in the West Indies. There, he regularly took students, friends, and tourists to the top of La Soufriere, the world's second largest active volcano, "just to see what happens at the top."

Dave Rodney on the summit of Mt. Everest, May 24, 2001.

When he returned to Canada, he spent a dozen years as an elementary school principal, a junior and senior high school teacher, and a coach. When he was not in the classroom, he hooked up with serious climbers. Mountaintops quickly became special places where he could relax and renew. "Everyone needs a sacred space. It doesn't matter whether it's a mountain or a monastery, a backyard or a bubble bath, as long as it enhances re-evaluation and re-creation."

A 1989 ski-jumping accident in Montana in which he tore his left knee apart and fractured two vertebrae could have put an end to his life on mountaintops. He could have used his injuries as an excuse to back away from the challenges ahead, but instead, he chose to see it as warning that he needed to gauge risk more carefully. "Life is not a spectator sport," he says.

His affair with Everest began in 1997 as part of a Canadian-American expedition. He did not attempt to climb to the summit, but shot video footage and delivered "Adventure Everest On-Line '97", an interactive website of his own design that allowed 300,000 students and the employees of two global businesses to follow the expedition and learn about the mountain. The effort won the team a City of Calgary special achievement medallion.

In the spring of 1999, Rodney returned to Everest as the climbing photojournalist for an international team. He reached the summit on May 13 and enjoyed 33 minutes on top of the world before he had to begin his trek back to base camp. "I am incredibly fortunate. Many have died in the effort to get to the top, and even more have perished on descent. We who have survived owe a debt to 'climb with a conscience' wherever we go."

The risks of such efforts are underscored during dangerous rescues. In 1997, he was part of a team that rescued a Sherpa who had fallen 150 feet down a crevasse. Miraculously, the man survived. In 1999, teammate Michael Matthews disappeared upon descent and there was nothing Rodney could do. In 2001, he was part of a team that recovered the body of Babu Chirri, one of the most famous climbing Sherpas of all time. The mountaineer had plunged to his death in a crevasse that had been hidden by a skiff of snow. "I'm not a rock jock with a death wish. I have a life wish, and I want to live it to the full. . . . Having looked death in the face, I cherish every single moment of everyday existence,

Kick-off for "Feed the Seed"
Shine-a-thon fundraiser.

knowing how close I have come to los-ing it all," Rodney says.

And he's using every minute as wisely as he can. Rodney launched his 2001 trip in the name of two charities: the Canadian Diabetes Association and the Light Up the World project. He chose the first charity in recognition of a friend, Steve Kelly, and an uncle, Emil Rudneski, both of whom have the dis-ease. The second choice was to focus attention on a Canadian initiative Rod-ney believes improves the lot of people in the Third World.

Instigated by University of Calgary professor Dr. David Irvine-Halliday, the project introduces safe, simple, healthy, reliable, rechargeable lighting systems to people who do not have access to what we consider a basic need—electricity. "I've seen Sherpas try to read by kerosene lamps and keep warm by yak-dung fires, inhaling deadly emissions in the process. We take lighting for granted; but for them, it's a luxury. This system, when introduced, raises the quality of living in even the most remote rural areas."

149

There are ups and down to everything in life, especially climbing. Rodney is still recovering financially from his three-month adventure in 2001, which cost him $30,000. He takes the bus around town because he sold his Mustang to help defray costs, but he's not complaining. In fact, he's considering a third attempt at reaching the summit with an American astronaut friend who has always dreamed of standing on top of the world. For Rodney, the trip will be an opportunity to produce a documentary about the Sherpa people, the unsung heroes of Everest. Before that, however, Rodney will complete a book using the mountain as a metaphor for life and conclude work on the documentary "Back to Everest: The Dave Rodney Story," a project of Partners in Motion, an Emmy Award-winning production company based in Regina.

"I've encountered all sorts of obstacles during my time in the mountains, and I am very grateful for them, since they have taught me that anything is possible with the right attitudes, actions, and resources. Surely, if a Prairie boy with a broken back and a reconstructed knee can scale Everest twice, each of us can achieve our own goals, whatever they may be."

This athlete supports:

Light Up the World
Department of Electrical &
Computer Engineering
University of Calgary
2500 University Drive NW
Calgary, AB T2N 1N4
website: www.lightuptheworld.org

Mustard Seed Street Ministry
102-11 & 106-11 Avenue SE
Calgary, AB T2G 0X5
website: www.theseed.ab.ca

Banded Peak Challenge
for Camp Horizon
website: www.bandedpeak.ca

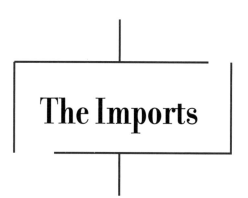

The Imports

Michael "Pinball" Clemons
Champion for Charities

BORN: JANUARY 15, 1965
DUNEDIN, FLORIDA

Too short, too small, too poor, too slow, too old, too inexperienced. At every twist of his incredible life, Michael Clemons has endured the labels and faced the obstacles. And at every turn, he has deftly weaved his way through, emerging brilliant, and smiling, always smiling—the most beloved and respected player ever to grace Canada's football fields.

With a grin as large as his career, Michael "Pinball" Clemons, the longest-serving Toronto Argonaut, is renowned as the Canadian Football League's most electrifying player and a man who gives as much off the field as on. Mention his name and you will hear as much about exceptional character as community awards, athletic excellence, and yards amassed; you will hear about a champion of causes and a champion on the field.

From a childhood of poverty in the housing projects of Dunedin, Florida, Clemons has become one of the most popular figures in Toronto's sports history. Soft-spoken yet enthralling, Clemons' wisdom, words, and indelible optimism are mesmerizing. Over the telephone, you can somehow hear him grinning.

Ask him about mentors, inspiration, heroes, or role models and he'll talk about one remarkable person: his mom, a shy, quiet women who taught him by example about hard work and giving. Ask him about his greatest accomplishment, and he'll say his family: wife Diane and two young daughters, Rachel and Raven.

Ask him about being a star and he'll tell you that, "It's nice to be important but it's more important to be nice. We can't all play pro football. We can't all be accomplished professionals. But we do all have an ability to give to our community. If you want to show me a great person, don't show me how much money he makes or how powerful he is or how many awards he's won or how many records he's broken. If you want to show me a great person, show me what he's done for someone else."

Now president of the Toronto Argonauts, Clemons began his CFL career when he signed as a free agent with the Argonauts in 1989. He would play for the team for the next 12 years, shattering records and setting new standards, before being made head coach in 2000 and then president of the Argonaut organization in 2001.

At only five feet six inches and 170 pounds, Clemons is an unlikely football dynamo who won over the most skeptical of skeptics dogging his path from the time he was a child. Growing up without a father, Clemons was raised by hard-working single mom, Anna Bryant, who was 18 when Clemons was born. Anna's mother had died when Anna was five, and she was brought up by her great grandmother, Annie Sinclair. By the time Clemons was born, Annie Sinclair was in her late 70s and blind. While Clemons' mother was raising a son, she was also looking after the woman who raised her.

"She never made excuses," says Clemons, whose childhood was rooted in the church. "She went to work. She sacrificed for me. And she did for others. She cooked for people, took care of people who were sick, gave people rides. If someone dropped off food to us, she'd bring it to the family next door, which had four kids." Anna Bryant began working for the City of Dunedin as a receptionist in the utility and billings department soon after Clemons was born. She's still there, now

Toronto Argonaut Mike "Pinball" Clemons is tackled by Montreal Alouette defensive back Mark Washington as Alouette cornerback Irvin Smith looks on.

supervisor of the department, and the first black person ever to rise to an administrative position.

While there were few luxuries growing up, Clemons says there was no shortage of love in his home, or discipline. He knew from an early age that he was expected to reach past his meagre beginnings and excel. He did. Clemons was only eight when he began playing football and it was obvious even then that the pint-sized kid had unusual talent. In high school, Clemons was all-state in football and soccer. He also earned the Principal's Award for academic achievement and citizenship.

He went on to earn a bachelor of arts degree in economics from College of William and Mary in Williamsburg, Virginia, where he carved out a top spot in the school's history, amassing 4,778 all-purpose yards and scoring 31 touchdowns in his four years at the college. In his senior year, he was team captain and Virginia College Player of the Year. The step up to the NFL saw Clemons play for the Kansas City Chiefs in 1987, reaching the Tampa Bay Buccaneers' camp the following year.

But it would be as a Toronto Argonaut with the CFL that Clemons would become "Pinball"—for his spec-

tacular moves that made it look as though he were bouncing and bopping off players like the frenetic little ball in a pinball machine. It would be as an Argonaut that he would amaze, delight and captivate fans. It would be as an Argonaut that Clemons would become the most productive player in pro-football history. He established all-time standards for all-purpose yardage in a career (25,402) and in a single season (3,840). He is the only player to surpass 5,000 career yards in four separate offensive categories—rushing, receiving, kickoff returns, and punt returns—and the only player to gain 1,000 yards in three separate categories in a single season.

He was the CFL's outstanding player in 1990, three-time Grey Cup champion (1991, 1996, and 1997), two-time CFL all-star (1990, 1997), and four-time division all-star (1990, 1993, 1994, and 1997). Among his numerous team records are most pass receptions in a career (682) and in a single season (122).

But the outstanding statistics are not what makes this football hero the legend he is today. His other statistics do that: the amount of time he spent on the field long after the game was over to meet young fans and sign autographs (hours), the amount of money he has

Toronto Argonaut "Pinball" Clemons hams it up with Patty Connors, the Special Olympics Female Athlete of the Year, at the Special Olympics Sports Celebrities Festival in Toronto, December 8, 1999.

raised for numerous charities (millions), and the number of causes he has supported (dozens).

While being tackled on the field, off the field Clemons was tackling such issues as violence, education, poverty, medical research, social services, and mental health, to name a few. Canadian Special Olympics, Canadian Cancer Society, United Way, Red Shield Campaign, Junior Diabetes Foundation, Big Brothers, Children's Miracle Network, Easter Seal Society, Athletes in Action, Down's Syndrome Association of Metro Toronto, and the Rising STAR program (founded by Clemons to promote self-control, forward thinking, a positive attitude, and respect in young people) are just some of the organizations that have benefited from Clemons' magnetism and humanitarian spirit.

Of all the accolades he has received, Clemons' most cherished awards have little to do with how far he ran with a ball, but with how far he has gone for those less fortunate. There's the Tom Pate Memorial Award for outstanding sportsmanship and dedication to the community (1993 and 1996); the Mayor of Toronto Celebrity Citizen Award (1997);

the John Candy Memorial Award (1995); the Canadian Council of Christians and Jews' Good Servant Award for outstanding community leadership; the ALS Iron Man Award, won three times; the Gordon Buwell Award for Exemplary Christian Character; and most prestigious, the Order of Ontario, presented to him in 2001.

More than football, says Clemons, it's the charity work that has taught him about real challenges, about pure joy, and about tireless dedication. "It's had a wonderful place in my life. It's taught me about being grateful for what I've been blessed with." It's difficult to take credit for what happens on the football field, he adds. "First of all, I was blessed with some God-given abilities. Then coaches give you opportunities, and then all the players around you help make it happen. The other things, the involvement in the community, are about choices, and these choices are the most significant."

A much sought-after speaker, Clemons recently made another choice: to become a Canadian citizen. He and his wife, now landed immigrants, hope to become citizens this year, cementing their commitment to their adopted community.

This athlete supports:
Canadian Special Olympics
60 St. Clair Avenue E, Suite 700
Toronto, ON M4T 1N5
e-mail: solympic@cso.on.ca

Vince Carter
Flying High

BORN: JANUARY 26, 1977
DAYTONA BEACH, FLORIDA

The man can fly. And while he's up there, he spins. Quite literally, Vince Carter walks on air. The NBA guard-forward, with his astonishing leaps, is in the midst of a media and fan love-fest that has sent his career soaring into the stratosphere of superstardom not seen since Michael Jordan walked on the court. Most exciting for Canadian basketball fans is the fact that Carter signed on with the Toronto Raptors through the 2007-8 season. He's ours, all ours. Instead of the warm waters of the Atlantic Ocean, home for one of the biggest sports stars in the world now overlooks chilly Lake Ontario.

But with nicknames such as the "Dunking Defender, the "Human Highlight Film," "Mr. Upside," "His Airness," and "Air Canada," how does this young sensation stay so grounded? And he is grounded. Only four years into his pro career, the 25-year-old has established himself as someone devoted to the community and, in particular, to kids with big dreams and little means to get there.

He's got his priorities straight," says Bev Deeth, executive director of the Raptor's Foundation. "He's a big guy with a big heart. Unlike many athletes, Vince has grown up focusing on giving

back." It comes from his mother, Michelle Carter, a retired teacher who is well known in her hometown of Daytona Beach, Florida, for reaching out to underprivileged kids. She was the teacher who would sneak out at lunch hour to buy a jacket for a child she noticed was coming to school without one. She was the mom who showed up at every game with the Gatorade and the banner.

Carter decided he wanted to do some giving himself when drafted into the NBA. With his mom, he created the Embassy of Hope Foundation. The name stems from a letter from a little boy who referred to him as an ambassador. The foundation held its first fundraiser—a golf tournament—in October 1998 in Daytona. "We had no money; Vince didn't even golf," recalls Michelle Carter with a laugh. "We figured, we'll just get the name out there, maybe break even." Carter bought clubs and people bought into the cause because it was Vince Carter. The foundation cleared $60,000. "We were knocked off our feet," recalls Michelle. That Christmas, the foundation handed out 105 food baskets, many of them delivered by Carter himself. It was a deeply moving experience for the

Toronto Raptor Vince Carter (right) drives past Memphis Grizzly Pau Gasol.

wealthy basketball star, and the Embassy of Hope grew.

The pair established Embassy of Hope Canada, based in Toronto. But Carter didn't stop there. He then created Vince's Hoop Group, a program that encourages students to succeed at school and in life; Vince Carter's Believing in Christmas, which makes the holidays special for needy families; and Vince's Jam, a series of charity events including an all-star basketball game and an all-star golf tournament. In 2001, Vince's Jam generated about $500,000 for youth at

risk across Ontario and for the Ronald McDonald House, Bloorview Mac-Millan Centre, and the Boys and Girls Club of Ontario. The basketball game attracted a raucous sellout crowd of 19,800.

"It comes from being raised by two teachers who would come home in the evenings and talk about how some parents weren't doing what we thought they should be doing for their children," says Michelle. "Listening to that year after year and noticing himself that parents may need help as well as their kids, it must have sunk in. It comes from within. It's part of him."

There's no doubt that the uncanny ability to handle a basketball also comes from within. Born January 26, 1977, in Daytona Beach, Florida, the six-foot six-inch, 225-pound Carter began showing outstanding basketball skills while in high school, where, it's been reported by the *Toronto Sun,* he was "as popular as spring break." Although he was offered a music scholarship to Bethune-Cookman College, Carter chose basketball and the University of North Carolina, where he became a star on the Tar Heels, the same team that gave birth to Michael Jordan's fame.

In 1998, after three seasons, 1,267 points, 466 rebounds, 197 assists, and helping his team compile an 83–22 overall win-loss record, Carter was drafted by the NBA. Selected fifth overall by the Golden State Warriors but traded to the Toronto Raptors for Antawn Jamison on draft day, Carter quickly transformed the Raptors into one of the top franchises in the NBA and the team to watch because of his dazzling performances.

He was named NBA Rookie of the Year after his first season with the Raptors and followed it up in 1999–2000 by finishing fourth in the NBA in scoring, averaging 25.7 ppg. In fact, 1999–2000 was a banner year for Carter, who was a sensation in winning the NBA Slam Dunk Contest, leading the U.S. team to the 2000 Olympics, and carrying the Raptors to the NBA playoffs for the first time in franchise history.

That same year, and for the next two, Carter received more votes than any other player for the NBA All-Star Game. In 2002, he surpassed Michael Jordan's vote count by nearly 500,000 votes, but didn't play in the game because of injury.

In each of his NBA seasons with the Raptors, Carter, with his thrilling moves, dynamic dunking, and acrobatic leaps, has led the team in scoring. In 2001, he topped the Raptors during the playoffs with an average of 27.3 points. He became the team's all-time leading scorer on March 2, 2001, surpassing Doug Christie's 4,448 points. He owns a career average of 24.6 points and 5.7 rebounds in 207 career games and was named Ontario's most outstanding athlete of 2001 with the Syl Apps Award, beating out homegrown greats like golfer Mike Weir and Maple Leafs goalie Curtis Joseph.

Carter is such a powerful engine for

the Raptors that when the engine stalled in February 2002 because of an injury, the team went into a nasty tail spin. Carter missed seven games. The Raptors lost all seven. He came back to do some damage control, but the hole was dug and the slump continued. The losing streak would last for 17 out of 18 games and Carter, paying the price of stardom, took much of the heat. The 2002 season ended prematurely for the star when it was announced in March that he would be undergoing arthroscopic surgery on his left knee.

Yet, for all Carter's athletic prowess, it was education, goal setting, and a fine balancing act that made him who he is today. With a mother and stepfather who were both teachers, his was a childhood in which writing poetry, playing saxophone, leading the high school marching band as a drum major, and earning a university degree were more important than shooting hoops. When Carter left the University of North

Carolina one year before completing his degree to join the NBA, his mother made him sign a contract stipulating he would continue his studies in the off-season.

Michelle Carter's proudest moment is said to be when Carter was handed his degree in African American Studies on a day last year when the rest of his team was practising for the biggest game of the season—playoff Game 7 of the Raptor's series against the Philadelphia 76ers. Carter flew to North Carolina the

Vince Carter addresses participants in Carter Summer Jam, July 30, 2001, at Ryerson Polytechnic University, Toronto, Ontario. Carter Summer Jam is a week-long series of fund-raising events supported by Carter's Embassy of Hope and the Raptors foundation.

163

morning of the game for the graduation ceremony and was back in time for the showdown. The team lost the game by one point.

But there's no doubt it's basketball that has made this well-rounded, gentle giant absolutely huge. Rich, too. The Toronto contract is said to be worth about $94 million, not including multi-million dollar endorsements. Yet it's his heart, not his head, that has grown with fame and fortune. Vince Carter, known to be quite shy, is not too big to hang out with a teenage girl struggling with cancer, just to chat. He's not so big that he doesn't hesitate to top up a Christmas fund he read about with a $10,000

gift. He's not so big that he doesn't call his mom almost every day.

"I have always told my son that one day, we're all going to walk away from this game of basketball for the last time," says a formidable Michelle, whose closeness with her son is nearly as famous as he is. "Relationships are the things that are lasting. That's what's important in life." And that's what keeps Vince Carter's flying feet firmly on the ground.

This athlete supports:
Embassy of Hope Canada
PO Box 51540
Toronto, ON M4E 1C0

Daniel Igali
From Poverty to Powerhouse

BORN: FEBRUARY 3, 1974
PORT HARCOURT, NIGERIA
BECAME A CANADIAN CITIZEN JULY 1998

Standing in a gymnasium at Burnaby's Simon Fraser University, Daniel Igali tasted the bitter sting of defeat for the first time. Soaking in a swirl of ugly emotions—loneliness, frustration, embarrassment—he vowed never to be unprepared again. With that simple decision, the 23-year-old wrestler took the single most important step in his long march from poverty in Nigeria to life as national sporting hero in two countries half a world apart. With it, the seeds of one of the most memorable triumphs in Canadian Olympic history were planted.

Not that it was the first time Igali had faced adversity. On the contrary, Igali's life to that point had been a series of mountains to climb. Along the way, he'd had plenty of role models to teach him the importance of believing in oneself and accepting the sacrifices one must make on the path to greatness.

Igali learned much about hard work and sacrifice from his grandmother, who worked to support Daniel and his siblings by fishing and labouring on farms in the countryside surrounding Port Harcourt, Nigeria. His parents had moved to England to study in hopes of improving their lot in life, and providing their family with a better standard of living. Igali spent much of the first 19 years of his life living under the same roof with 20 other brothers, sisters, and cousins as his grandmother struggled to feed them two meals a day.

"We slept a few to a bed, and a few of us shared food on a plate," Igali remembers now. "But I cherish those memories." What formal education was available had to be fought for, and Igali carried his own desk to school everyday. His family had already instilled in him the importance of an education. For most, it was the only path out of poverty. But some of his most valuable lessons were learned in the schoolyard, grappling with other children, proving his wrestling prowess in a country where the sport is revered.

By the time Igali was a teenager, his extraordinary wrestling talent had become obvious. In 1990, at the age of 16, he made his first appearance at the Nigerian national championships, wrestling against competitors in their early 20s. He had been training formally for less than a year, but he managed to win the national championships, against all odds. By 1993, he was the African champion and seemingly on his way to serious international success.

Preparing for the Commonwealth

166

Canada's Daniel Igali competes at the 2000 Sydney Olympic Games.

Games in Victoria, B.C., in 1994, Igali let himself daydream about the possibility of staying in Canada. It would mean leaving behind the family who were so important to him, as well as the minor-celebrity status he'd attained at home. But Igali was troubled by the political instability back home and was desperate to get the education he needed to leave his days of poverty behind him. He also knew that his only hope of becoming a truly great international wrestler, capable of winning Olympic gold, was in the coaching and facilities available in the West.

Two days before the games were to conclude, Igali made his decision. Aided by a volunteer driver named Tom Murphy, who opened his home to the young wrestler, Igali slipped away from the Nigerian team officials and applied for refugee status in Canada. "I decided to stay in Canada because I saw no future in Nigeria," Igali says. "I was willing to gamble that staying in Canada would afford me the future that I wanted: to go to school, have a degree, and compete to my highest capability. That is all I wanted."

The gamble was soon paying big dividends. When Igali enrolled at Simon Fraser University (SFU), he began work with wrestling coach Mike Jones, and his Olympic dreams came sharply into focus. Igali reamed off an incredible 116 consecutive wins over three years at SFU, and was soon among the most feared competitors in his division.

Away from the wrestling ring, things were not so easy. In Nigeria, Igali's only exposure to Canada was what he saw in brief snippets on CNN. Having been granted refugee status in 1995, Igali expected that he would quickly become one of the country's prized Olympic hopefuls and would be given an apartment, a car, and funding to support his development. He was unprepared for the massive culture shock that awaited him in B.C., and everything from the cold weather to the difficulty most Olympic athletes face paying for their training regimens. He washed dishes, picked berries, babysat children, and worked in construction to pay the bills. It all left Igali painfully homesick. "I never expected to be as lonely as I felt," Igali says. "In the first couple of years, I got really tempted to go back home."

Perhaps the most important person to help Igali overcome the day-to-day adjustments to Canada was Maureen Matheny, a former school teacher and principal, and mother-in-law of his closest friend, Idris Orughu. She became a surrogate mother for Igali, and the one person he knew he could rely on for anything. And he would need all the support she could give him after Igali faced defeat that day at SFU in the finals of the 1996 Clansman International tournament.

Igali was wrestling a well-respected veteran of the sport named Terry Steiner. Igali had jumped to a commanding 7–1 lead in the match with just one minute remaining on the clock. Igali was tired and feeling confident the match was his, and that gave the cagey Steiner the opening he needed. He scored six points in the final minute, forcing the match into overtime, where he defeated a shaken Igali. "I lost that match before I even stepped on the mat," Igali says now. "I decided never to be embarrassed the way I was that day, from that day forward."

Igali immediately intensified his training schedule, lifting more weights and driving himself in cardiovascular exercise. He scraped together what little money he had to buy a video camera to tape every one of his matches. He pored over the tapes for hours, looking for flaws, finding ways to improve. Out of the ashes of that embarrassing defeat, Igali made his major step into the elite of the sport. In 1998, he placed fourth at the World Championships in Tehran, Iran, and second at the World Cup tournament. In 1999, he won his first world championship in Ankara, Turkey. But his ultimate goal was still Olympic gold.

Through all his highs and lows, Maureen Matheny was there. But she would not see the ultimate step in Igali's spectacular journey. In 1999, after a long fight with cancer, Matheny died, just five days after Igali was crowned world champion. The wrestler was crestfallen, but resolved that the death of his surrogate mother would drive him even harder towards victory at the 2000 Olympics in Sydney, Australia.

"Maureen was an angel sent from heaven to teach me the values of true friendship," he says. "Though I was devastated after she died, after sober reflection, I am convinced that God brought her into my life to teach me that true friendships and love do not have to be blood-related. [She] always made me realize that everything was possible, but more importantly, that everything happens for a reason."

It was that sense of Matheny's strength that went into the ring with Igali as he competed in Sydney in the 69-kilogram weight class. Going into the games, Igali was unknown to most Canadians, but that would soon change, as his skill in the ring and engaging enthusiasm in interviews endeared him to the people of his adopted country.

When Igali defeated Russia's Arsen Gitinov in the gold-medal match, the eyes of the country were focused on Igali and he became an instant national hero. As Igali danced around the ring in celebration, his overjoyed coach grabbed him and threw him to the mat. When Igali got back up, he grabbed a Canadian flag, draped himself in it, then laid it on the mat, kneeled down, and kissed it. Igali explained later that he had an acute sense that day that Canada had won that medal with him. Without the support of people like Matheny and the coaching of people like Mike Jones, the moment he'd dreamed about since he was a child growing up in the swampy Nigerian delta would never have come true.

Igali's celebration galvanized a feeling

of national pride in a country that rarely makes an open show of patriotism. Igali's display of overflowing joy was contagious. Broadcast around the world and featured on the front pages of most of the country's newspapers, it made him an instant celebrity and offered Canadians a rare moment of sporting glory at an Olympics that had been a disappointment for many.

What most people didn't know was just how far Igali had come for that victory, and what odds he'd had to defy.

Igali had overcome poverty, politics, and more than a little pain in pursuit of greatness. Now, as he quickly became a household name across Canada, Igali began to look for ways to use his new-found fame to give back to the people and places that had helped him on his journey.

Igali decided that with all the wealth surrounding him in Canada, and the admiration he'd earned at the Olympics, he needed to find a way to build a school and gymnasium back in his old

Daniel Igali wins the Norton H. Crow Award—Canadian Male Athlete of the Year in Toronto, Ontario, March 20, 2001.

hometown of Eniwari, Nigeria, where his family still lives. He soon joined forces with Matheny's son, Kevin, a high school teacher in B.C. who had followed his mother into the education profession. Kevin enlisted the support of his students, and with Igali's help, they are working to raise $200,000 to help kids in Nigeria pursue the educational and athletic success for which Igali had fought.

With the support of Igali's corporate sponsors, Cheerios and RBC Financial Group, the project seems to be headed for success. But Igali's determination to make a difference in Nigeria didn't end there. He has created the Daniel Igali School Project, a charitable fund he hopes will provide steady funding for the maintenance of that country's crumbling schools as well as for the creation of education programs that will spread the word about dangers ranging from domestic violence to HIV and AIDS, which claim thousands of lives in Africa every year.

"I remember, growing up as a kid, having to carry my desk to school, not having shoes, having the rain pour down on me, even while in class," Igali says. "I am determined to see that younger chil-

dren do not go through the same tribulation that I faced as a youngster."

When the school is built, it will stand as a monument to the connection between two countries half a world apart, and as a reminder of what can happen when friends set their minds and talents to a goal. And it will bear an appropriate name: Maureen Matheny School.

In early July 2002, Igali was named flag-bearer for the Canadian team at the Commonwealth Games in Manchester, England. Although coaches advised him to skip the event, and prepare instead for the world freestyle championships in Iran in September, he said he needed to be there since it's likely to be his last shot at the Games.

"It will be very befitting," he told the Canadian Press. "I don't want to start talking about an end to my career because I'm not finished competing, but if I never compete again I will be very satisfied that I went to the Commonwealth Games for Canada."

This athlete supports:
Daniel Igali School Project
13727 93A Avenue
Surrey, BC V3V 8A9

Chris Reitsma
Pitcher with a Purpose

BORN: DECEMBER 31, 1977
MINNEAPOLIS, MINNESOTA
RAISED IN CALGARY, ENJOYS DUAL CITIZENSHIP

It was a rainy August day in Stoney Creek, Ontario, the start of the Canadian Big League championships. The best of the country's teenage baseball players had gathered, like they do every year, to compete for the national title. The uncooperative weather meant a 15-minute rain delay, but now the Calgary Blues were back on the field in the small park warming up. The mound was being repaired, the infielders and outfielders were playing catch to warm up, and Chris Reitsma was getting ready to pitch.

Suddenly, a violent boom rocked the diamond, an explosive crack Reitsma will never forget: "It was right on top of us." The lightning bolt's current ripped through the wet grass, knocking everyone off their feet. Eerily, 16-year-old Reitsma was the only one left standing. His feet were planted on the pitching rubber. "I was in tears. I didn't know what to do," Reitsma recalls. "I ran to our shortstop and his hat was burned. He couldn't talk but he pointed to left field. I looked up and Matt Krol wasn't moving at all."

Young Matt Krol died that day in 1994. Several players were treated in hospital for irregular heart rhythms. Eight years later, the strange and tragic incident still doesn't seem real to Reitsma. He thinks about Matt Krol a lot, usually when he's on the pitcher's mound, always when he sees dark clouds on the horizon.

He looks for those dark clouds all the time. No longer playing in small fields in small towns, Reitsma scans the horizon from the mounds of the biggest and best diamonds of Major League Baseball. A rookie pitcher with the Cincinnati Reds, Reitsma doesn't know what made him get back on the mound after that August day. He just knows he's meant to play baseball, and he's making every minute count. As long as the skies are clear.

"It's the one thing I can't deal with —seeing a storm rolling in. I see it and I get spooked. I freeze. I see it and I think of Matt. Once, in Cincinnati, there was a storm coming in. I wasn't playing, thank goodness. I was on the bench. I got up and had to walk into the tunnel to the clubhouse. It hasn't happened while I've been pitching, but I think if a storm ever got close and I was on the mound, I would call a time out. I don't care how important the situation. I'd walk off the field. I'm pretty sure."

From his home in Calgary where he spends the off-season, Reitsma is

Cincinnati Reds starting pitcher Chris Reitsma pitches during the second inning against the St. Louis Cardinals at Busch Stadium in St. Louis, Missouri, June 26, 2001.

passionate about the game that has thrown him more than one curve ball. His is a story of freak accidents and injuries, coming back when no one thought he could, and searching the horizon not only for storm clouds but for opportunities to make a difference in the lives of others.

Reitsma was born December 31, 1977, in Minneapolis, Minnesota, where his father, a pastor, was serving in a church. Originally from Lacombe, Alberta, Reitsma's father moved the family to Fresno, California, when Reitsma was a baby. They settled in Calgary when he was 11 to be closer to home.

Throughout high school, Reitsma

was a little league baseball star at the provincial and national levels. He pitched for the Canadian Junior National Team in 1995. His talent was huge, and upon graduating from Calgary Christian High School in 1996, Reitsma became the first draft pick by the Boston Red Sox, 34th overall. At the time, he was the highest-drafted Canadian ever in the Major Leagues.

But it would be nearly two full seasons before Reitsma's dream would begin to take shape. The six-foot five-inch, 214-pound pitcher was in for a devastating test of his strength and spirit. Before he could make it out of the Boston farm system, his elbow fractured in mid-pitch during a 1997 game. It happened again the following year. "After the second time, the doctor said I probably wouldn't be able to come back," recalls Reitsma. "I remember sitting there. I'm 20 years old and wondering what I was going to do with my life. Baseball was all I wanted to do."

The months ahead were filled with doubt and loneliness. "There was a time everyone gave up on me. I was a high prospect and suddenly everyone stopped calling, everyone stopped seeing how I was doing because they thought I was done." But Reitsma wouldn't give up. "I had this feeling that I had to give it one more try. I put my mind to it. I thought, if it breaks again, I'm done—I'm meant for something else. But I had to try it one more time."

His injury dropped Reitsma to single-A level with the Florida State League, but 2000 was a big year. "I got healthy, made some big jumps," he says. Traded to the Reds in the fall of 2000, Reitsma surprised those who had stopped calling by making starting pitcher out of spring training. He followed it up with an eye-popping major-league debut in April 2001, which earned him National League Pitcher of the Week (April 9–15). The league

referred to his performance as "nothing short of outstanding," as he went 2–0 in his first two starts, giving up just one earned run on 11 hits and four walks in 13.1 innings. He managed nine strike-outs, defeated the Pittsburgh Pirates in that team's first regular-season game at their new PNC Park, and threw seven shutout innings against the New York Mets on April 14.

Chris Reitsma, with his mid–90 mph fastball and exciting changeup, was once again a brilliant pitching prospect. He would end the 2001 season with a respectable 5.29 ERA, lead Major League Baseball with most innings pitched by a rookie (182), establish himself as one of the league's top rookies, and become the only pitcher in major-league history to come back from two broken elbows.

Now married to high school sweetheart, Janelle, and first-time father to Kylie, born October 7, 2001, Reitsma, 24, is confident and excited about the coming season, when he will have to prove himself all over again. Yet he's also prepared for the dream to end. While in Cincinnati, he rents an apartment month to month, as rookies do. He thinks about continuing his work with mentally disabled young adults, a sideline he has enjoyed in the off-season

Cincinnati Reds catcher Jason LaRue (right) consoles pitcher Chris Reitsma in the third inning after the Philadelphia Phillies score five runs in the inning, April 12, 2002, in Philadelphia.

while volunteering for Rehoboth Christian Ministries in Calgary. The young handicapped men, to whom he has been a buddy—taking them to sporting events and simply hanging out with them—fascinate him, he says. They teach him about joy.

It's late January and the high in Calgary is minus 22 °C. Reitsma is snuggled inside his home with his wife and baby daughter. He loves being at home, even in a cold snap. Spring training is a week away. "Our families are here," he says of his hometown. "You can look from sky to sky and see blue the whole way. The mountains are looking right at you. It's a great place to raise a family."

It's a great place to think. When asked to speak at schools, church, and elsewhere, Reitsma encourages people to do just that—to think about their purpose in life, about where they can find strength, about how they are living their lives. "I have a strong belief we all have a purpose," says the gracious ball player. "I believe I'm here to use the gifts God has given me to the best of my ability. I've been given the ability to throw a baseball, so I'm going to do the best I can with it. And hopefully, through the platform I've been given, I can reach others and make a difference."

It's Reitsma's way of being ready, should lightning strike.

This athlete supports:
Rehoboth Christian
Ministries Foundation
3920–49th Avenue
Stony Plain, AB T7Z 2J7
e-mail: wally.mulder@rehoboth.ab.ca

The Barrier Breakers

Willie O'Ree
Hockey's Black Pioneer

BORN: OCTOBER 15, 1935
FREDERICTON, NEW BRUNSWICK

Four decades after Willie O'Ree skated his last shift in the NHL, the stocky 66-year old still laces up his skates and goes into the corners with the biggest names in the league. Unlike his shifts with the Boston Bruins in 1958 and again in 1961, when his colour made him the target of name-calling, spears to the stomach, and cross-checks to the head, the scrambles in the corner today are filled with laughter and the games are about fighting racism, not fostering it.

The first black man to skate in the NHL says his precedent-setting 45 games in the big leagues are important. But he believes that trailblazing effort is dwarfed by the work he's doing with young people today as director of the non-profit NHL/USA Hockey Diversity Task Force.

Designed to introduce children of diverse ethnic backgrounds to the game of hockey, the task force programs target economically disadvantaged children of all age levels. "It's not just about hockey. It's about life. It teaches life skills, and hockey is the mechanism," he exhorts with the fire of an evangelical preacher. "This program stresses education, education, and education. These kids will not play hockey forever, but they can use the skills that they learn about life forever and that is what I try to teach."

Polite, dignified, and well-spoken, O'Ree has logged nearly 500,000 kilometres flying between NHL cities, offering on-ice workshops with big-name minority players such as Grant Fuhr, the storied netminder who has won four Stanley Cups; Edmonton's Anson Carter; and Carolina's Kevin Weekes. During his travels, O'Ree also speaks in schools, using his own life as an example of how determination can overcome adversity.

Born in 1935, O'Ree honed his hockey skills on the frozen ponds and rivers of Fredericton, N.B. He laced on his first skates at age three and was playing in a local hockey league two years later. He said he felt free on skates and recalls spending 10 to 12 hours a day just working the puck up and down a backyard rink built by his dad.

There were only two black families in Fredericton at the time, and he says he never encountered racism while growing up. All his friends were white. And like him, they all dreamed of playing in the NHL. "The fact that I was black never came up when we played as kids," O'Ree wrote in his autobiography, *Hockey's Black Pioneer*. "You could

WILLIE O'REE

Although O'Ree never had a player card during his brief NHL stint, two cards with his picture and game stats have been released in recent years in recognition of his pioneering role in hocky.

have been purple with a green stripe down the middle of your forehead, and it wouldn't have mattered. It was only later, when I became older, that I learned what 'colour barrier' meant."

A speedy left-winger with dazzling agility, O'Ree became one of the best players in New Brunswick. In 1954, he was invited to join the Quebec Frontenacs of the Quebec Junior Hockey League for the princely sum of $60 a week. He impressed coaches and players alike with his talent and his nothing-can-stand-in-my-way attitude, but his dream of NHL glory almost vanished during his second year in the league. While playing a game with the Kitchener-Waterloo Canucks, he was hit in

the face with a puck. He lost 95 percent of the vision in his right eye and doctors told him to quit.

He refused. He kept his blindness a secret and was back on the ice within eight weeks.

Helmets were still rare at the time, so he went back without one. But when he talks to kids today, he cringes to think about the risk he took. He is a firm advocate of helmets and face shields and promotes an NHL used-equipment-bank program, which provides young, economically disadvantaged players with full gear.

O'Ree turned pro in 1956 and played for the Quebec Aces, a Quebec Hockey League team affiliated with the Boston Bruins. It was there that he got his first taste of the racism he would face every time he stepped onto the ice for the rest of his career. He was taunted in the corners, spat at, and had drinks poured on him while he sat in the penalty box. There were terrible stick fights and, more than once, he had to chase an obnoxious fan back into the stands.

When he recalls those dark moments,

at sessions for young minority players who play in borrowed shin guards and scuffed helmets, he says he needs to tell such tales so the kids can make sure it doesn't happen to them. "I didn't allow myself to get sucked in by [racists]. I wasn't going to let a bunch of ignorant, stupid people chase me away from hockey. You shouldn't either . . . I never once fought because of a personal racist insult," he says proudly. "If I fought every time I received a racist remark, I would have done nothing but fight."

During his second season with the Aces, O'Ree got the call he'd been waiting for. The Bruin's lineup was in shambles and the team needed him to replace an injured player. On January 18, 1958, he made history when he donned a black-and-gold uniform and made his NHL debut against the Montreal Canadiens.

Great fanfare had accompanied Jackie Robinson's breaking of the colour barrier in professional baseball 10 years earlier, but to O'Ree's surprise, the official integration of hockey garnered little attention. "I thought it would get a little more publicity than it did," he said. "But people were used to seeing me play in Montreal, so the press treated it like it was just another piece of news . . . I didn't care about it myself, but it could

have been an important touchstone for other blacks with hockey ambition. I always imagine a young black kid playing extra hard because it had been shown a black could make it."

O'Ree played a second game against Montreal before he was shipped back to Quebec. The experience whetted his appetite for more, so he redoubled his effort with the Aces. Although legally blind, he rejoined the Bruins in 1961 and played 43 games, scoring 4 goals and notching 10 assists.

If the media didn't make a big deal about him being the first black man to play in the NHL, some of the other players did—in a bad way. He recalls a game in Chicago when Eric Nesterenko called him "nigger" and butt-ended him in the mouth, knocking out two teeth and breaking his nose. Determined not to be run out of the rink, O'Ree retaliated and opened a 15-stitch gash on Nesterenko's head. The benches cleared and the fans went wild. When Chicago officials were unable to guarantee they could control the fans, O'Ree spent the rest of the game locked in the Boston dressing room, for his own safety.

After the 1961 season, O'Ree was traded to Montreal and then to the Los Angeles Blades of the Western Hockey

League. It would be another 16 years before another minority player, Washington Capital Mike Marson, played in the NHL.

O'Ree spent a dozen years playing with the Blades and the San Diego Gulls, leading the league in goals in 1964–5 and again in 1969, at age 34. He had hoped to return to the NHL during the six-team expansion in 1967, but the call never came. He figures that by that time, most people in hockey knew he was blind in one eye and couldn't pass the NHL vision test.

O'Ree retired from professional hockey in 1979 without much fanfare, and his achievement might have remained little more than a footnote in hockey history if it hadn't been for Bryant McBride, the NHL's vice-president of business development and a member of the NHL/USA Hockey Diversity Task Force.

McBride was in charge of getting more minority players into the league and in 1996 wanted to bring 24 kids from different ethnic backgrounds to play in a special tournament in Boston. He wanted to call it the Willie O'Ree All-Star Weekend, with O'Ree as a featured guest. O'Ree loved the opportunity to work with kids and was invited again the following year, when the event was held in Chicago. In 1998, he was not only invited to the party but also invited to join the task force, as director.

His new role made him a mentor to thousands and earned him notoriety for his pioneering effort. A film was made about his life, he's been profiled on sports channels, and in 2000, he penned his autobiography. O'Ree has also been instrumental in getting $500,000 worth of used hockey equipment donated to minority hockey

Willie O'Ree speaking at the Truro Sports Hall of Fame dinner in Truro, Nova Scotia, on February 28, 2002.

teams and has encouraged athletes to donate autographed souvenirs which have been sold off to raise an additional $250,000 for hockey programs.

The NHL is still more than 90 percent white, but O'Ree believes that is changing. There were approximately 28 minority players on the 2000–01 NHL regular season rosters, but he sees lots of minority talent ready to break through. "I'm proud to have the opportunity to give back to the game of hockey,"

O'Ree says, "and try to touch as many young people as possible. The barriers I faced are down now. If you really set your mind to it, you can make it."

This athlete supports:
NHL Diversity Task Force
National Hockey League
1251 Avenue of the Americas, 47th Floor
New York, NY 10020

Brian MacLeod
Shooting in the Dark

Born: May 9, 1959
Truro, Nova Scotia

Brian MacLeod shakes out his arms and adjusts his grip on the driver. There's a moment of complete stillness, and then the 43-year-old Nova Scotia resident unloads on the golf ball. A small gaggle of onlookers bursts into applause as the ball rockets 250 yards and bounces twice before stopping in the dead centre of the fairway. "How'd I do?" MacLeod asks coach James Wallace earnestly. The white dimpled ball is plainly visible to the small gallery, but MacLeod can't see it. He's blind.

"Just because I can't see, doesn't mean I can't golf," says MacLeod, accepting the seven-iron Wallace passes for the coming approach shot. "'Can't' isn't in my vocabulary. It shouldn't be in anyone's, no matter what challenges they face."

As one of Canada's best blind golfers, MacLeod has faced his share of obstacles. In addition to his blindness, complications resulting from diabetes have necessitated two transplant operations that have left him with enough track-like scars to run a short-line railway. But with the determination of a Tiger Woods, or Mike Weir, he's chipped out of the sand traps life has dealt him and is sinking clutch putts to win trophies he's able to feel but never see.

Blind golf has been around for about 20 years in Canada, with players competing in predetermined sight classifications ranging from totally blind, like MacLeod, to those with 6 to 10 percent vision. Play takes place on the same courses as sighted golfers and follows the same rules, except that blind golfers are allowed to ground a club in sand traps so they know where the ball is. Like a PGA player with a caddy, each player has a coach who helps line him up, tells him the distance to the pin, and describes the shot. After that, the golfers are on their own.

At 5 feet 10 inches and 190 pounds, MacLeod is a leftie who hits 150 yards with his eight-iron and consistently smacks his drives 240–50 yards. His best round since losing his sight is 97, and he generally shoots in the low 100s. Wallace believes with more international tournament experience, MacLeod could easily be shooting in the mid-90s.

The 2001 season provided ample evidence of his talent. MacLeod won tournaments in California and Hamilton, Ontario, and had top five finishes in Birmingham, Alabama, and Carlisle, Georgia. He qualified for the 2002 World Championships in Winnipeg and was invited to play in a tournament in Ireland.

"Brian is among the top five to seven

best totally blind golfers in the world, " says Dennis McCulloch, a director of the International Blind Golf Association living in Winnipeg. "He has an excellent game. He's got a shot at the top spot in whatever tournament he enters."

But getting to tournaments is not easy. There are few sponsors in blind golf and no financial jackpot in tournament wins. The fees are a burden, but MacLeod is willing to pay out of his own pocket because golf is the one game where he can still compete against others. "And like every athlete, I want to challenge myself against the best," he says.

Growing up in rural Nova Scotia, MacLeod thought golf was a sissy game. Real athletes played baseball and hockey, he thought, so he set out to emulate them. He always played forward on the rep teams in community hockey leagues and was a starting pitcher in the local hardball circuit. His first game of golf came at age 14 when he opted to tag along with a friend rather than return home to do some long-neglected chores. From his very first shot, he was hooked.

"It was meant to be," he explains. "It was like grudgingly going on a blind date and finding the girl of your dreams. After my first round, I couldn't get enough. I'd play one course in the morning, another in the afternoon, and then play baseball in the evening." But at age 16, his energy level dropped like a ball in a water hazard. He used to jump out of bed for a predawn skate; now his mother had to drag him out of bed for school. The change was dismissed as "a lingering flu" until one day he passed out while walking down the stairs.

Blind golfer Brian MacLeod gets aligned by coach Fraser Nicholson during a round of golf.

187

Incoherent and near death, he was rushed to the hospital, where a battery of tests determined he was one of over two million Canadians with diabetes.

If left untreated or improperly managed, the high levels of blood sugar associated with diabetes will slowly damage blood vessels. Diabetes is a leading cause of adult blindness, and people with diabetes account for 28 percent of all new cases of serious kidney disease.

"I was devastated," MacLeod says of the diagnosis. "Daily insulin shots and a strict diet shouldn't have been a big deal, but it made me feel like I was different. It felt like I had a big dark secret. I didn't tell my friends about it."

MacLeod is frequently asked to speak with young people with diabetes. He tells them trying to hide it is the worst thing they can do. By keeping it to himself, the disease became like a stone tied around his neck that grew heavier every day. The heavier it got, the harder he tried to prove he was physically fine. As a result, he didn't look after himself. He believes it was this neglect that led to his blindness, at age 27.

MacLeod's interest in hockey and baseball diminished as his love of golf grew. In 1985, he won three local tournaments and worked his handicap down to eight. By the end of the season, he decided it was time to start competing at higher levels and bought himself new set of clubs. He never got a chance to use them.

As quickly as his diabetes had seemed to strike, so did his blindness. Within four months, he went from haziness in one eye to complete and permanent blackness. The cause: Diabetic retinopathy, the bleeding of small blood vessels in the back of the eye. As MacLeod accepted his blindness, he unwittingly surrendered his dreams. Without thinking, he donated his skates and hockey sticks to a kid in the local league and sold off the new clubs. Who'd ever heard of a blind guy playing golf?

Luckily for him, a pro at a nearby course had. In 1986, during one of his regular visits to a golf shop where he went to reminisce and caress club heads, he was confronted by Jim Crowdis. "He told me I didn't need to see the ball to hit it. He said if I just kept the front arm straight, it would always come back to the same position where it started. He was right. I just have to have to concentrate on mechanics big time. I can't be moving my body."

Inspired, MacLeod returned to his

Brian MacLeod speaking to a Sunday School class at St. John's Anglican Church in Truro, Nova Scotia.

beloved links and began beating down his handicap. He was just rediscovering his rhythm when his health failed again. His kidneys gave out and he was forced to spend eight months on dialysis waiting for a donor organ. Transplants of this sort were tougher a decade ago than they are now. But after two years of rejection problems and recuperation, MacLeod was able to once again tee up the ball. He played recreationally for three seasons before he felt ready to test himself in competition.

In his first tournament, the 1997 Blind Canadian Open, MacLeod placed fourth in his division. It was a huge confidence boost and he began hoping for big things in 1999, at the biannual tournament in Saskatoon. He practised hard, but as the tournament neared, it was clear his transplanted kidney was failing. He played anyway and placed a disappointing seventh, but says now he didn't remember some of the holes immediately after playing them.

In July 2000, he was fortunate to get a second transplant—this time both a kidney and a pancreas. Not only did the operation save his life, it freed him of the symptoms of diabetes that had sapped his energy. "I felt a little bit like a gutted fish," he says with the same wry humour he uses to make students comfortable when he talks to school groups about the challenges of blindness and diabetes. "But just three weeks out of hospital, with 50 staples in my belly, I was back on the course swinging a golf club. It hurt, but I was determined not to back down."

Since that time, MacLeod has been playing regularly, winning tournaments and, as president of the Colchester Visually Impaired Recreation Association, encouraging more blind people to take

189

up the game. "For the blind and visually impaired, golf can be a great way of getting them integrated into society and helping them boost their self-esteem," he says. "It won't put an end to the waitress who yells at the blind because they think they must be deaf or the people who treat us like we are fragile china that's ready to break, but seeing a blind guy sink a putt from 10 feet may change a few minds."

This athlete supports:

Canadian Diabetes Association

National Office

15 Toronto Street, Suite 800

Toronto, ON M5C 2E3

Chantal Petitclerc
Chasing Challenges

BORN: DECEMBER 15, 1969
ST. MARC DES CARRIÈRES, QUEBEC

Chantal Petitclerc has been on the go since 3 a.m. She was up before dawn to read a sportscast for CBC's Radio-Canada. Then she tossed the wheelchair into the car and was off to a local Montreal school to speak to several classes of kids. After a quick supper, it was off to Loto-Quebec to present the evening's lottery results on TV. She does all this while she's getting over jet lag from a recent trip to Australia, a country dear to her heart because that's where she attained her goal in life—her most recent one, anyway. She won gold—and several other medals—at the 2000 Paralympics, and says it was the proudest moment of her life.

Petitclerc had an impressive record going in to the games. She had already won five medals at the Paralympics four years earlier. But she constantly sets new challenges for herself. And while Petitclerc entered five events in Sydney, her main goal was to unseat Australia's perennial 800-metre champion, Louise Sauvage.

Petitclerc's greatest strength is her starts, and she knew that's where she held the advantage. She bolted from the starting line to claim the lead that would put her on the top of the podium, though that most-treasured victory was almost wrestled away from her because of a crash well back in the race. Officials were going to rule the results invalid, but since it didn't affect the outcome of the race, her gold was upheld several days later.

After being named Female Athlete of the Year for 2001 by Sports-Quebec, a nonprofit umbrella organization of 60 sporting federations, Petitclerc said it was the best race of her life. "To be the first to defeat Australia's Louise Sauvage on her home turf and to see the extremely gracious reaction of local sports fans towards me are moments that I'll always cherish."

You might think that would be enough. But not for Petitclerc. She topped the podium again in the 200-metre and added a pair of silver medals, all at the one games. Petitclerc is known for her solid determination. That sense of perseverance which emanates from soft brown eyes that simply shine with a zest for life. Petitclerc has had several roadblocks put in front of her over the years, but has simply seen them as challenges to be met head on and overcome.

Petitclerc was just 13 years old when her life changed forever. She was playing at her friend's farm, trying to lift a

Canada's Chantal Petitclerc competes in an athletics event at the 2000 Sydney Paralympic Games.

broken barn door, when it fell on her, rendering her paralyzed for life from the waist down. "It was a stupid accident," she says, matter-of-factly. She took life one day at a time, first dealing with the pain and then teaching herself how to sit, dress, and eat again. It wasn't until a few months later that the reality of her changed life hit her.

But she never felt sorry for herself. She just reconciled herself to the fact that this was the way her life would be, and she was going to go ahead and live it to the fullest. "It wasn't overly catastrophic for me. I had good people around me. I don't remember the accident so much; I keep memories of good things. My progress was very fast, I wanted to regain my autonomy. I had my ups and downs but I don't remember being depressed. I saw it more as a challenging time."

The accident didn't make her a determined person—Petitclerc says she already was. "You don't become something else because of an accident; it becomes the basis for certain qualities to come out." Petitclerc skipped out of rehab early and was back in school within a few months. She believes that's what helped her get strong so quickly. "It gave me a vision that I could keep doing the same things, have the same friends in my life. Things were different but not stopped."

She couldn't take part in regular gym classes, but her teacher, Gaston Jacques, suggested she take up swimming to build her strength. That again boosted her confidence as she realized she could still lead a vibrant life. Petitclerc then added weight training to her regimen, and that's when wheelchair-racing coach Pierre Pomerleau spotted her, at age 17. Petitclerc was working out at the Francois-Charon Rehabilitation Centre in Quebec City. Pomerleau told

Abilities Magazine, "There was nothing outstanding about her physically. What struck me was her determination."

At age 18, she entered, and won, her first race. The prize for Most Promising Athlete was a racing wheelchair. She went on to set a world record in the 100-metre and has proven her versatility by taking numerous medals in the 100-, 200-, 400-, 800-, and 1,500-metre races.

One of Petitclerc's goals along the way is for people to overcome their view of wheelchair racing as a disabled sport: "People have to see it as just a sport and the wheelchair is a piece of equipment, the same as a bicycle or a kayak. It is a legitimate sport, you know." She's made progress. People used to be filled with amazement at her courage. Today, Petitclerc said they want to know about the technical aspects of the sport, her best time, and her top speed (32 kilometres/hour).

Kids are particularly curious, and blunt. They want to know about her accident, if she has a boyfriend, and what he's like. It's important to her to spend time with young people, but she's careful in her approach. "I don't preach to them; I want to share my experience and hope they will recognize something in that and want to pursue it in their own lives."

She tells kids they have to have guts and be willing to take risks: "We all have a passion in life for something and it's important to believe in it. Sometimes we have a goal that's bigger than ourselves." But that's no reason not to reach it; in fact, she says, it's even more reason to work harder and reach higher. Petitclerc particularly enjoys working with physically and mentally challenged children through an annual sporting event he called Le Defi Sportif.

It's been 13 years since Petitclerc began racing, and she still loves it. She races for the pure enjoyment of the sport, but she says it's also a way to learn about yourself. "It taught me a lot about having my dreams, setting goals, achieving them, and that's one of the things that stays with me." Attitude is as important as being physically prepared for a race: "You have to be positive, you have to keep your motivation and stay disciplined. Those are things you learn on the track, but you bring them to other aspects of your life."

It might be difficult for an athlete whose coach lives in another city to stay focused. But not for Petitclerc. She trains by herself up to six hours every day, doing weights and stationary training (on her chair, set up on rollers), and wheeling

Team Canada's Chef de Mission Wayne Hellquist (left) and Chantal Petitclerc (centre) attend a news conference at the 2000 Sydney Paralympic Games.

on an indoor track in the winter and racing on an outdoor track when the weather is better. She keeps in touch with trainer Peter Eriksson by e-mail and phone, and visits whenever she can. Ericksson described her in an interview with *Abilities Magazine* as "probably one of the most outstanding athletes in Canadian history," wheelchair or not.

So what's next on Petitclerc's to-do list? "My goal is still very clear," she says. "Right now, my goal is to go to Athens [in 2004]. I won two silver and two gold in Sydney, and I want to be able to maintain that level of performance." Just as important is her broader goal. "I still hope [wheelchair racing] will finally be recognized as an official sport at the

Olympics. That's one of the main reasons I continue. I really want to see this sport become an Olympic sport and to be there when it is."

Petitclerc once said, "An Olympic medal is worth more to me than an Paralympic medal. I'm not hiding it— I'm doing everything I can to win." It's galling to her that bridge is an official sport at the Olympics whereas wheelchair racing is not, but, once again, Petitclerc sees this as yet another challenge. She hasn't let one slip by her yet.

This athlete supports:
Le Defi Sportif
525 Dominion Street, Office 340
Montreal, QC H3J 2B4

Photo Credits

Cover: (top left, Gretzky) CP Photo/Mike Ridewood; (top centre, Laumann) CP Photo/COA; (top right, Hansen) CP Photo/COA/J. Merrithew; (bottom left, Wickenheiser) CP Photo; (bottom centre, Stojko) CP Photo/Paul Chiasson; (bottom right, O'Ree) NHL/ The Upper Deck LLC Company. 3: CP Photo/Kevin Frayer. 5: CP Photo/Mike Ridewood. 6: CP Photo/ Edmonton Sun/Brendan Dlouhy. 9: CP Photo/Phil Snel. 11: CP Photo. 12: CP Photo/Toronto Sun/Warren Toda. 16: Terry Fox Foundation/Gail Harvey. 19: Terry Fox Foundation/Gail Harvey. 20: CP Photo/Bill Becker. 23: CP Photo/AP/Ed Andrieski. 24: CP Photo/AP. 26: CP Photo/COA. 27: Rick Hansen Man in Motion Foundation. 29: CP Photo/COA/J. Merrithew. 31: CP Photo/Toronto Star/Boris Spremo. 35: CP Photo/Paul Chiasson. 37: CP Photo/AP/Katsumi Kasahara. 39: CP Photo/Toronto Star/Bernard Weil. 41: CP Photo/Regina Leader Post/Bryan Schlosser. 43: CP Photo/Chuck Stoody. 45: CP Photo/Saskatoon Star Phoenix/Leslie Parreaux. 47: CP Photo/Peter Bregg. 49: CP Photo/Boris Spremo. 51: CP Photo/ Toronto Star/Colin McConnell. 53: CP Photo/ Toronto Star/Frank Lennon. 55: CP Photo/Toronto Star/David Cooper. 57: CP Photo/John Lehmann. 59: CP Photo/Hans Deryk. 61: CP Photo/COA. 62: CP Photo/Toronto Star/Ron Bull. 65: CP Photo. 67: CP Photo/COA/R. Warren. 69: Alberta Adolescent Recovery Centre. 71: CP Photo/AP/Steven Senne. 73: Sun Media Corporation. 74: Cam Neely Foundation. 79: CP Photo/Aaron Harris. 81: CP Photo/Kevin Frayer. 83: CP Photo/Toronto Sun/Zoran Bozicevic. 85: CP Photo/Adrian Wyld. 87: CP Photo/Frank Gunn. 89: CP Photo/Paul Chiasson. 91: CP Photo/ Aaron Harris. 93: CP Photo/AP/Adam Butler. 95: CP Photo/Aaron Harris. 98: CP Photo/Jeff McIntosh. 99: CP Photo/COA/Mike Ridewood. 101: CP Photo/ Adrian Wyld. 103: CP Photo/COA/Claus Andersen. 105: CP Photo/COA/Ted Grant. 107: CP Photo/Fredericton Daily Gleaner/Diane Dioron. 109: CP Photo/Frank Gunn. 111: CP Photo/COA/Mike Ridewood. 113: Kids Help Phone. 114: CP Photo/ COA/Claus Andersen. 116: CP Photo/Adrian Wyld. 118: CP Photo/Ryan Remioriz. 120: CP Photo/COA/ Ted Grant. 122: CP Photo/COA/Ted Grant. 124: CP Photo/Clement Allard. 129: Sun Media Corporation. 131: CP Photo/COA. 133: CP Photo/Frank Gunn. 134: CP Photo/Phil Snel/Maclean's. 137: CP Photo/Tom Hanson. 138: CP Photo/Andrew Vaughan. 140: CP Photo/Tom Hanson. 142: CP Photo/COA. 144: CP Photo/AP. 145: Michael Matthews. 147: Jen Rodney. 149: Jen Rodney. 153: CP Photo/Frank Gunn. 155: CP Photo/Paul Chiasson. 157: CP Photo/Toronto Star/Vince Talotta. 159: CP Photo/Aaron Harris. 161: CP Photo/Aaron Harris. 163: CP Photo/Andrew Stawicki. 165: CP Photo/ Ryan Remiorz. 167: CP Photo/COA. 170: CP Photo/Salvatore Sacco. 172: CP Photo/Calgary Herald/David Lazarowych. 174: CP Photo/AP/James A. Finley. 176: CP Photo/AP/Rusty Kennedy. 179: Steve Proctor. 181: NHL/The Upper Deck LLC Company. 183: Steve Proctor. 185: Steve Proctor. 187: Steve Proctor. 189: Steve Proctor. 191: CP Photo/La Presse/Pierre McCann. 193: CP Photo/ COA/Jean-Baptiste Benavent. 195: CP Photo/COA/ Jean-Baptiste Benavent.